Name _____

One More of Each

Work with a partner.

1. Draw 17 △'s.
Ring 10.

How many left? _____

2. Draw 18 ○'s.
Ring 11.

How many left? _____

3. Draw 19 □'s.
Ring 12.

How many left? _____

4. Draw 20 X's.
Ring 13.

How many left? _____

Do you have the same amount left each time?
Tell your partner why.

Name _____

A New Coin

Work with a partner.
Look at the coins.

1. Tell what is different about  and .

2. Tell what is different about and .

3. Make a new coin.
   Draw it. Give it a name.

4. Compare your coin to a  , , and .
   What is the same?
   What is different?
   Share your ideas with your partner.

Name _____

Cover with Cubes

How many cubes will cover each space?
Write an estimate. Use cubes to check.
Write how many.

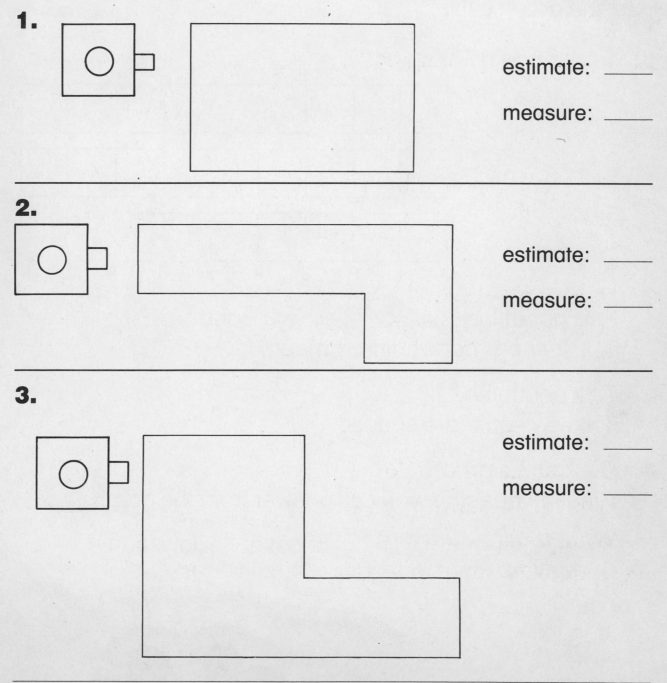

1.

estimate: _____

measure: _____

2.

estimate: _____

measure: _____

3.

estimate: _____

measure: _____

Name ____________________

Play Ball

Work with a partner.
Look at the graph.
Tell what the graph is about.
Give the graph a title.

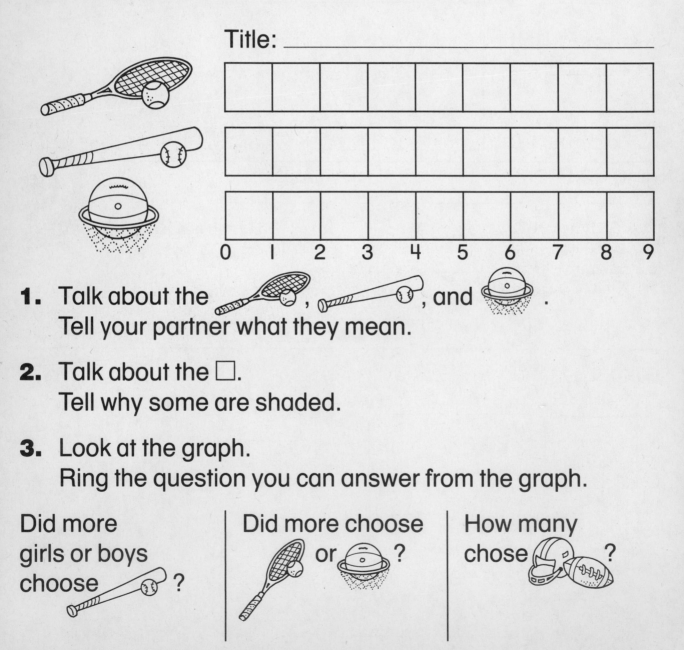

Title: ____________________

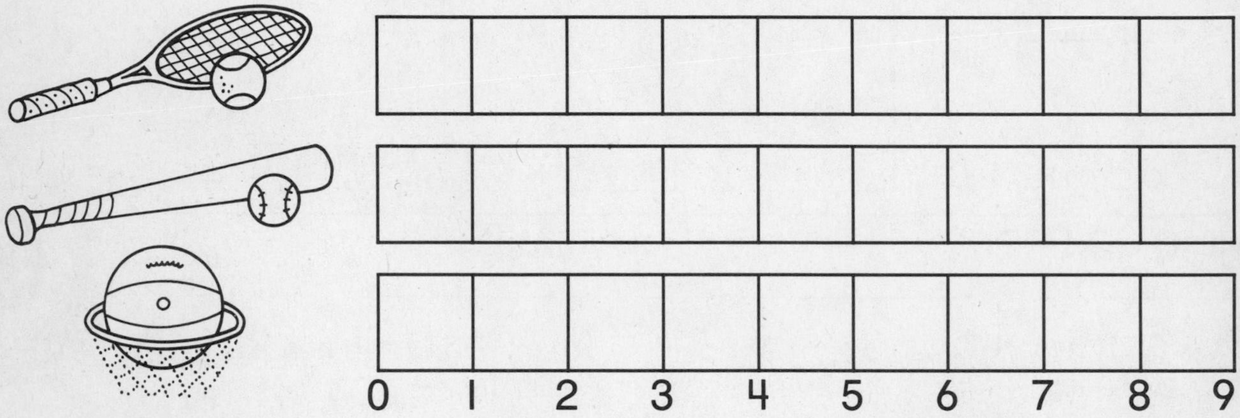

1. Talk about the , 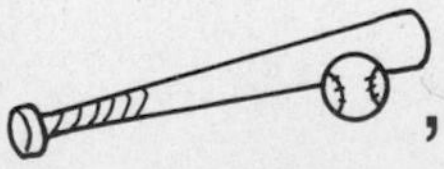, and .
Tell your partner what they mean.

2. Talk about the □.
Tell why some are shaded.

3. Look at the graph.
Ring the question you can answer from the graph.

Did more girls or boys choose 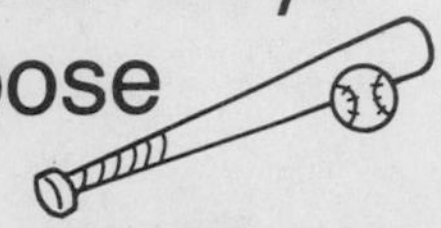?	Did more choose  or ?	How many chose ?

Name _____

Vacation Time

> Dear Family:
> Our class has been learning about numbers to 20 and graphing. Read the following story together. Help your child find the information in the story, then complete the graph.

16 students in first grade went on vacation.

Lisa, Kim, Tom, Su, Mark, and Megan went to Florida.

Ann, Jim, Tony, Scott, and Shari went to Arizona.

David, Sean, and Mario visited their friends in Texas.

Jean and her cousin Joann went to California.

Make a tally to show how many students went to each state.

Arizona _____   Texas _____

Florida _____   California _____

Color the graph to show the tallies.

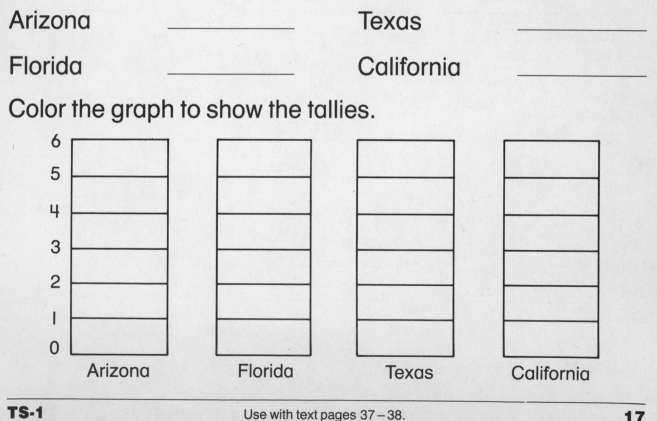

Name _____

Putting Things in Order

Write 1, 2, 3 to show the story in order.

1.

___   ___   ___

2.

___   ___   ___

3.

___   ___   ___

Use with text pages 39–40.

Name _____

Story Pictures

Read the story.

Find the picture that shows the story.

Color the picture to match the story.

The 3 blue birds sit in a tree.

The 2 brown squirrels play under the tree.

The yellow sun is high in the sky.

The 5 red flowers are by the tree.

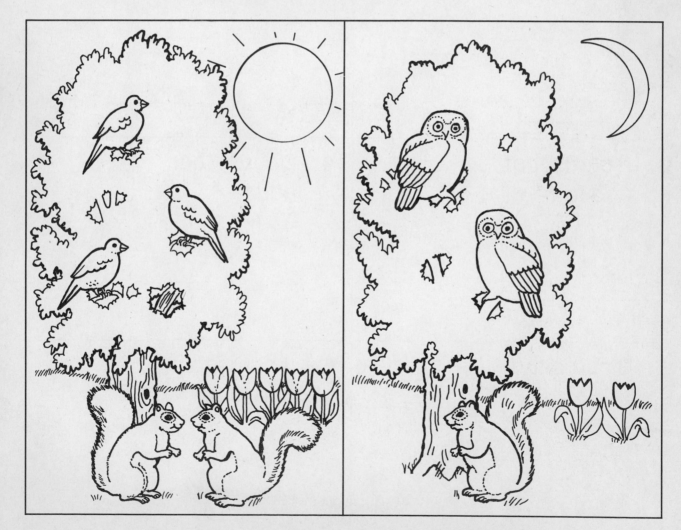

Name _____

Count and Check

Make number cards like these:

| 1 | 2 | 3 |
| 4 | 5 | 6 |

Use cards and counters for help.
Follow the directions.
Show the cards. Write how many in all.

1. 2 cards that
add to 5

☐ + ☐

_____
in all

2. 2 cards that
add to 7

☐ + ☐

_____
in all

3. 2 cards that
add to 6

☐ + ☐

_____
in all

4. 2 cards that
add to 8

☐ + ☐

_____
in all

5. 3 cards that
add to 6

☐ + ☐ + ☐

_____
in all

6. 3 cards that
add to 8

☐ + ☐ + ☐

_____
in all

Name _____

Addition Stories

Dear Family,
   Our class has completed a lesson on adding two numbers. Help your child cut and paste numbers to create addition sentences to show each sum. Then ask your child to tell a story about each addition sentence and talk about his or her answers.

Cut out each ☐.
Use ☐ to show the sum.
Paste. Tell a story
about each sentence.

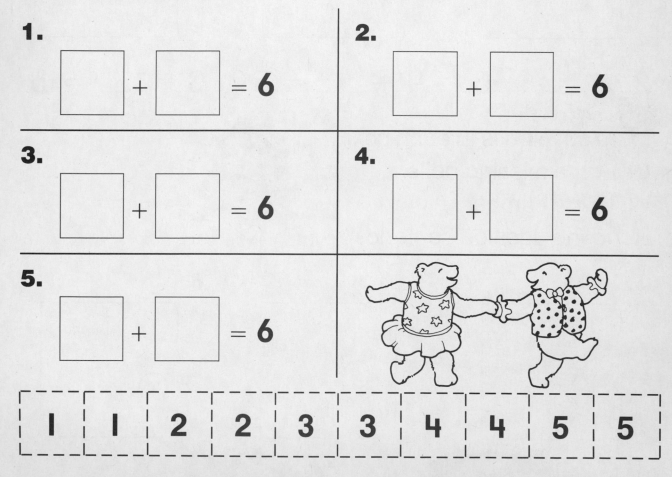

1.

☐ + ☐ = **6**

2.

☐ + ☐ = **6**

3.

☐ + ☐ = **6**

4.

☐ + ☐ = **6**

5.

☐ + ☐ = **6**

| 1 | 1 | 2 | 2 | 3 | 3 | 4 | 4 | 5 | 5 |

Name _____

Missing Balls

Paula put 5 balls in each box.
Draw the missing balls.
Write the number.
Read the addition sentence.

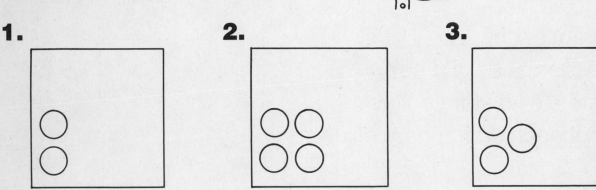

1.

2 + ___ = 5

2.

4 + ___ = 5

3.

3 + ___ = 5

Marc put 6 balls in each box.
Draw the missing balls.
Write the number.
Read the addition sentence.

4.

4 + ___ = 6

5.

3 + ___ = 6

6.

1 + ___ = 6

Name _____

Different Dots

Look at the dot cards.
Which one has a different number than the others?
Draw an X on the one that is different.

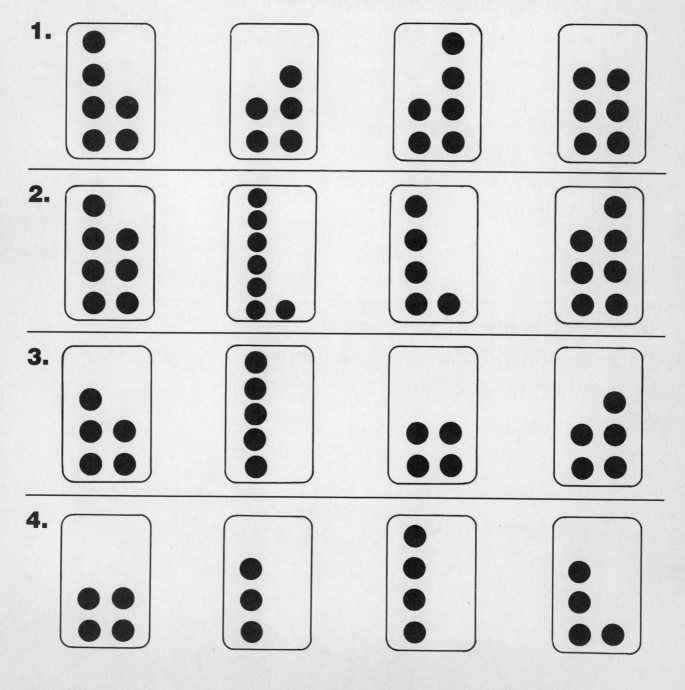

Name _____

Reach In

Pretend that you can reach in each jar.

1. Reach in the jar and get 5 buttons. How many black buttons do you think you would get?

_____ black

2. Reach in the jar and get 10 beads. How many white beads do you think you will get?

_____ white

3. Reach in the bank and get 5 coins. How many dimes and how many pennies do you think you would get?

_____ dimes   _____ pennies

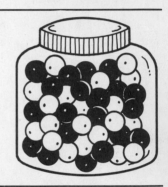

Name _____

What Does Not Belong?

Add. Cross out the fact that does not belong.

2 + 3 = ____
2 + 2 = ____
3 + 2 = ____

4 + 0 = ____
0 + 4 = ____
5 + 0 = ____

1 + 4 = ____
1 + 5 = ____
5 + 1 = ____

4 + 3 = ____
3 + 3 = ____
3 + 4 = ____

Name _____

Correcting Lucy!

Use a [calculator] to check Lucy's paper.

Ring facts with wrong sums.

1.
```
  4      3      2      2      4
+ 2    + 3    + 3    + 1    + 3
─────  ─────  ─────  ─────  ─────
  6      7      5      3      7
```

2.
```
  0      3      3      1      3
+ 6    + 1    + 4    + 1    + 2
─────  ─────  ─────  ─────  ─────
  5      2      7      2      6
```

3.
```
  5      1      2      1      5
+ 0    + 3    + 4    + 2    + 1
─────  ─────  ─────  ─────  ─────
  5      4      5      3      6
```

Write each fact that you circled.
Write the correct sum.

```
 +      +      +      +      +
───    ───    ───    ───    ───
```

Name _____

Pennies in the Purse

Work in small groups.

Guess how many pennies will fit.

Listen to each guess.

Then ring what you think.

Use punchout pennies to see.

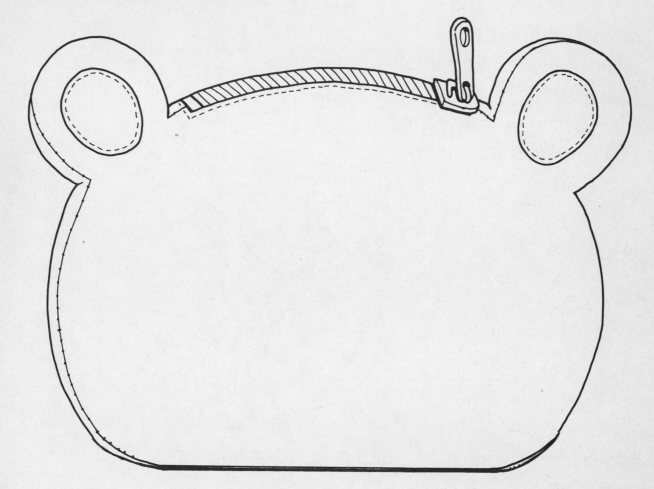

About   5   10   20   pennies

Critical Thinking

Name _____

Carrot Contest

Read the clues.
Write the rabbits' names in
order, to show how many
carrots they ate.

Five rabbits had a
carrot-eating contest.
Bill ate the most carrots.
Nan ate more than Jan.
Nan ate less than Dan.
Will ate less than Jan.

You can draw pictures
or act it out to help.

most carrots

_____

_____

_____

least carrots

Use with text page 63.   TS-1

Name _____

How Many Times?

Spin.
Show that many counters.
Take away 1.
Write what you do.

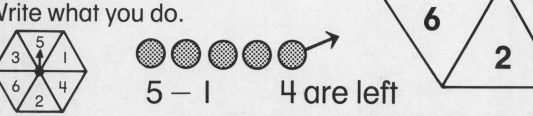

5 – 1   4 are left

	start with	take away	are left
1.	_____	----- 1	_____
2.	_____	----- 1	_____
3.	_____	----- 1	_____
4.	_____	----- 1	_____
5.	_____	----- 1	_____
6.	_____	----- 1	_____

7. How many times were 3 left? _____ times

8. How many times were 0 left? _____ times

Name _____

Can You Tell?

How many are inside?

1. 3 in all

┊ inside

2. 4 in all

_____ inside

3. 3 in all

_____ inside

4. 5 in all

_____ inside

5. 4 in all

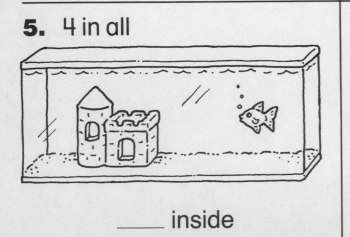

_____ inside

6. 5 in all

_____ inside

Name _____

At the Store

Guess what was bought to give the change.
Ring your guess.
Use a 🖩 to check.

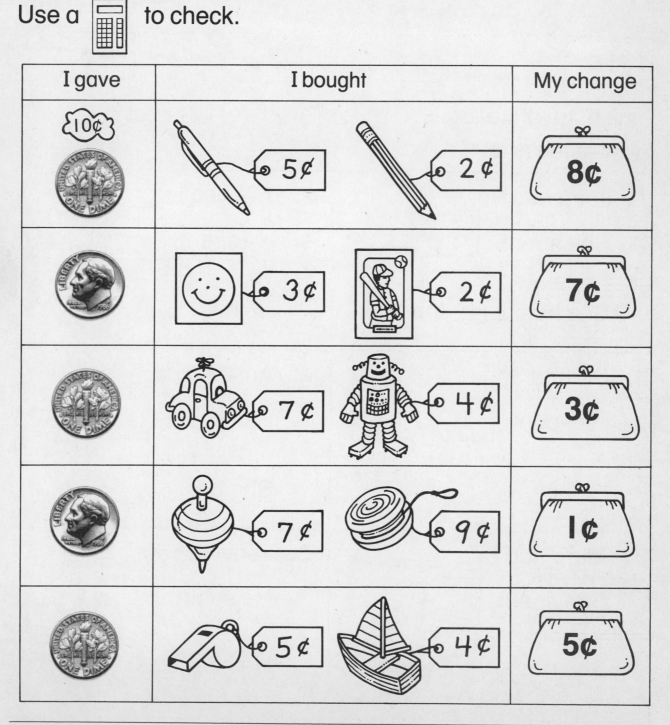

I gave	I bought		My change
10¢	5¢	2¢	8¢
	3¢	2¢	7¢
	7¢	4¢	3¢
	7¢	9¢	1¢
	5¢	4¢	5¢

Name _____

Buying Toys

1¢   **2¢**   **3¢**   **4¢**

Finish the price tag.
How much is left?

---

1. Jean had 4¢.

She spent ⌇ 1 ⌇ ¢

She has 3 ¢ left.

2. Tim had 5¢.

He spent

He has _____ left.

---

3. Bill had 3¢.

He spent

He has _____ left.

4. Ann had 6¢.

She spent

She has _____ left.

---

5. Mara had 5¢.

She spent

She has _____ left.

6. Tony had 5¢.

He spent

He has _____ left.

Name _____

Leaving the Nest

How many got away?
Use counters to act it out.
Write the number.

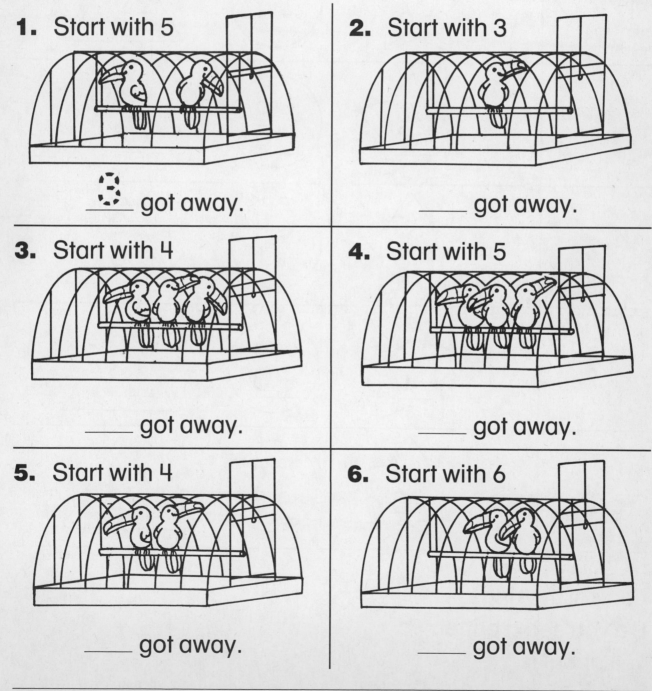

1. Start with 5

_3_ got away.

2. Start with 3

____ got away.

3. Start with 4

____ got away.

4. Start with 5

____ got away.

5. Start with 4

____ got away.

6. Start with 6

____ got away.

Name _____

Identifying Equivalent Expressions

Ring the ways to make each number.

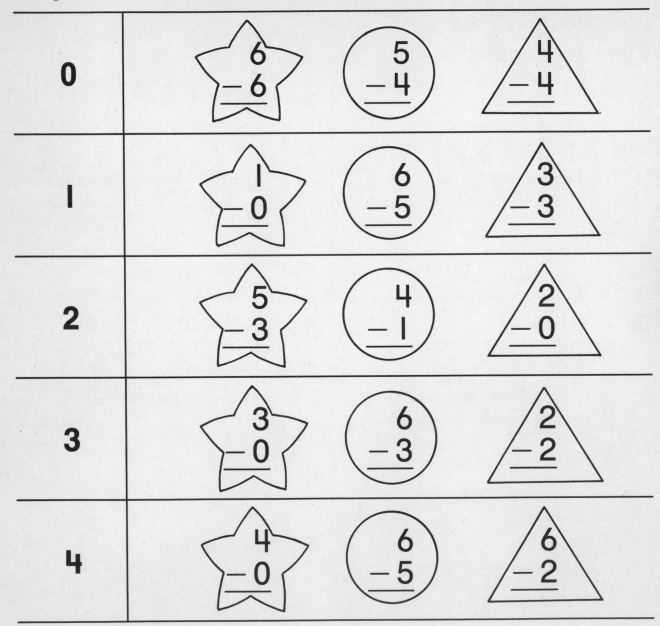

Look at the rings.
Do you see a pattern?
Tell about it.

Use with text pages 79–80.

Name _____

Discriminating Between Facts

Complete the facts in each group.
Ring the facts that are related.

1. (5 − 2 = 3)

5 − 4 = 1

(5 − 3 = 2)

4 − 1 = 3

2. 3 − 2 = ___

4 − 1 = ___

3 − 3 = ___

3 − 1 = ___

3. 3 − 1 = ___

6 − 1 = ___

6 − 5 = ___

6 − 3 = ___

4. 3 − 1 = ___

4 − 0 = ___

4 − 3 = ___

4 − 1 = ___

5. 4 − 0 = ___

4 − 4 = ___

4 − 3 = ___

3 − 0 = ___

6. 6 − 2 = ___

4 − 2 = ___

6 − 1 = ___

6 − 4 = ___

Name _____

Constructing Fact Families

Work in groups of 4 to make fact families.

1. Make cards like these:

| 4 | 5 | 1 | + | − | = |

Move them around to make a fact family.
Each person makes one fact.
Write number sentences to show the fact
family your group made.

___ + ___ = ___   ___ − ___ = ___

___ + ___ = ___   ___ − ___ = ___

---

2. Use these cards to make another fact family.

| 6 | 4 | 2 |

___ + ___ = ___   ___ − ___ = ___

___ + ___ = ___   ___ − ___ = ___

---

3. Use these cards to make 2 fact families.

| 3 | 3 | 6 | | 4 | 4 | 8 |

___ + ___ = ___   ___ + ___ = ___

___ − ___ = ___   ___ − ___ = ___

Name _____

What Have We Here?

Ring the number sentence for the picture.

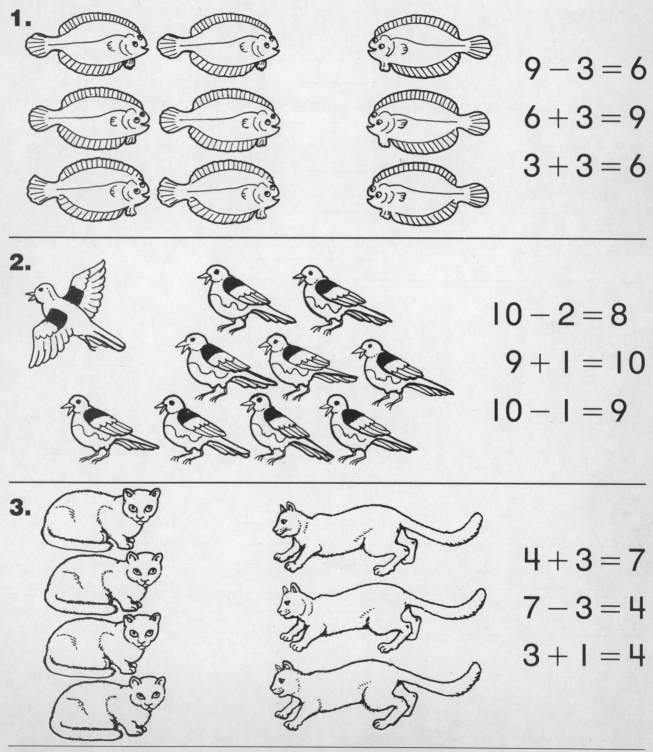

1.

$$9 - 3 = 6$$
$$6 + 3 = 9$$
$$3 + 3 = 6$$

2.

$$10 - 2 = 8$$
$$9 + 1 = 10$$
$$10 - 1 = 9$$

3.

$$4 + 3 = 7$$
$$7 - 3 = 4$$
$$3 + 1 = 4$$

Name _____

How Many Were Added?

Draw dots to show how many were added.

Begin	Add	End
1. 3 dots		5 dots
2. 2 dots		3 dots
3. 5 dots		6 dots
4. 8 dots		8 dots
5. 6 dots		8 dots
6. 9 dots		10 dots
7. 7 dots		9 dots
8. 4 dots		4 dots

Name _____

What Goes Up

1. 7 balloons   Draw 2 more.   How many are there now?

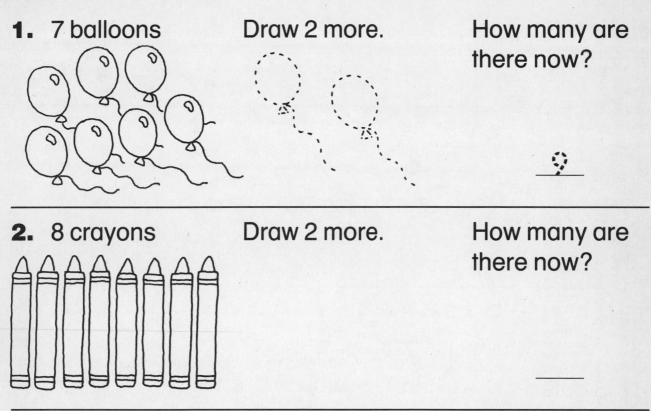

_9_

---

2. 8 crayons   Draw 2 more.   How many are there now?

_____

---

3. 9 balls   Draw 2 more.   How many are there now?

_____

---

4. 7 kites   Draw 3 more.   How many are there now?

_____

Name _____

Adding on a Number Line

Draw the jumps.
Add.

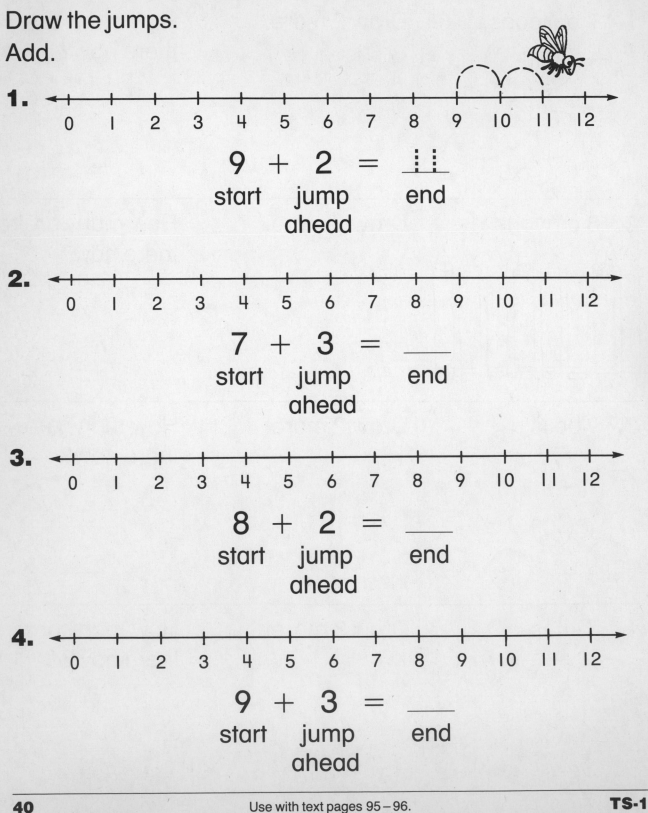

1.

0 1 2 3 4 5 6 7 8 9 10 11 12

9 + 2 = ¦¦
start   jump   end
        ahead

2.

0 1 2 3 4 5 6 7 8 9 10 11 12

7 + 3 = ___
start   jump   end
        ahead

3.

0 1 2 3 4 5 6 7 8 9 10 11 12

8 + 2 = ___
start   jump   end
        ahead

4.

0 1 2 3 4 5 6 7 8 9 10 11 12

9 + 3 = ___
start   jump   end
        ahead

Name _____

Missing Numbers

Count on 1, 2, or 3 to find the missing numbers.
Write the numbers. Check with counters.

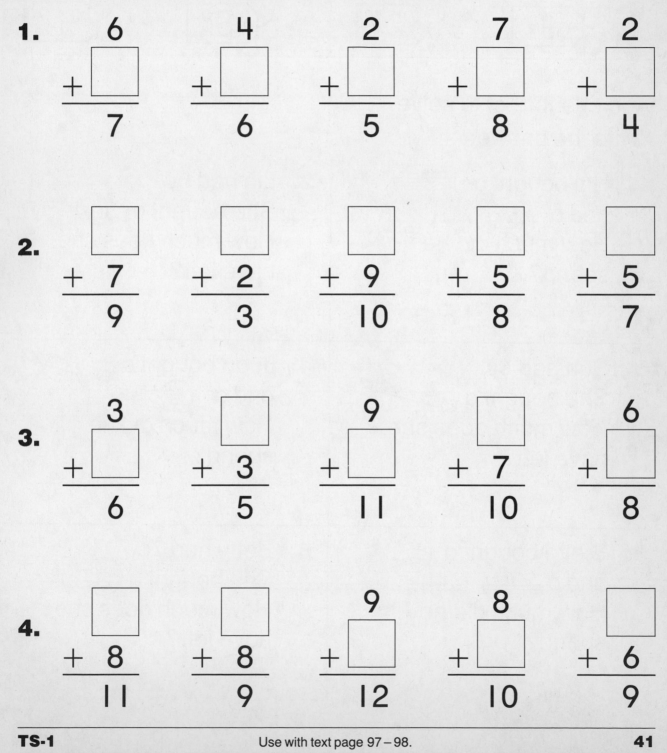

1.
$$\begin{array}{r} 6 \\ + \square \\ \hline 7 \end{array}$$
$$\begin{array}{r} 4 \\ + \square \\ \hline 6 \end{array}$$
$$\begin{array}{r} 2 \\ + \square \\ \hline 5 \end{array}$$
$$\begin{array}{r} 7 \\ + \square \\ \hline 8 \end{array}$$
$$\begin{array}{r} 2 \\ + \square \\ \hline 4 \end{array}$$

2.
$$\begin{array}{r} \square \\ + 7 \\ \hline 9 \end{array}$$
$$\begin{array}{r} \square \\ + 2 \\ \hline 3 \end{array}$$
$$\begin{array}{r} \square \\ + 9 \\ \hline 10 \end{array}$$
$$\begin{array}{r} \square \\ + 5 \\ \hline 8 \end{array}$$
$$\begin{array}{r} \square \\ + 5 \\ \hline 7 \end{array}$$

3.
$$\begin{array}{r} 3 \\ + \square \\ \hline 6 \end{array}$$
$$\begin{array}{r} \square \\ + 3 \\ \hline 5 \end{array}$$
$$\begin{array}{r} 9 \\ + \square \\ \hline 11 \end{array}$$
$$\begin{array}{r} \square \\ + 7 \\ \hline 10 \end{array}$$
$$\begin{array}{r} 6 \\ + \square \\ \hline 8 \end{array}$$

4.
$$\begin{array}{r} \square \\ + 8 \\ \hline 11 \end{array}$$
$$\begin{array}{r} \square \\ + 8 \\ \hline 9 \end{array}$$
$$\begin{array}{r} 9 \\ + \square \\ \hline 12 \end{array}$$
$$\begin{array}{r} 8 \\ + \square \\ \hline 10 \end{array}$$
$$\begin{array}{r} \square \\ + 6 \\ \hline 9 \end{array}$$

Name _____

Toy Sale

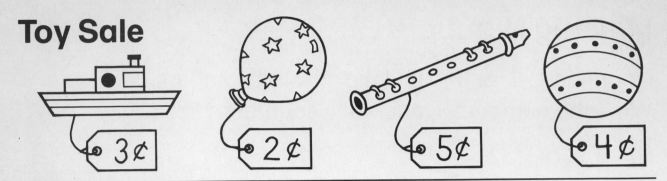

Add or subtract to solve.
Write the answer.

1. Hal bought a 🚢
and a 🎈.
How much did he
spend?

_____ ¢

2. Lin had 5¢.
She bought a 🎈.
How much does she
have left?

_____ ¢

3. Sue had 6¢.
She bought a 🪈.
How much does she
have left?

_____ ¢

4. Juan bought a 🪈
and a 🎈.
How much did he
spend?

_____ ¢

5. Steve bought a ⚽
and a 🚢.
How much did he
spend?

_____ ¢

6. Betty had 7¢.
She bought a ⚽.
How much does she
have left?

_____ ¢

Name _____

Button Toss

Work with a family member.

Toss a 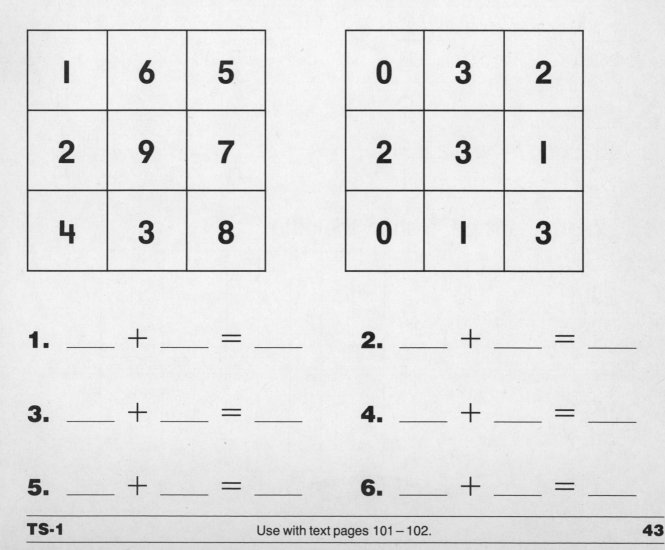 on each board.

Add aloud. Then write the fact below.

1	6	5
2	9	7
4	3	8

0	3	2
2	3	1
0	1	3

1. ___ + ___ = ___   2. ___ + ___ = ___

3. ___ + ___ = ___   4. ___ + ___ = ___

5. ___ + ___ = ___   6. ___ + ___ = ___

Name _____

Answer Check

Check Cathy's paper. Use ✔ for right answers.
Use X for wrong answers.

1.
$$8 + 1 = 9 ✓$$
$$6 + 2 = 7 X$$
$$9 + 1 = 10$$
$$7 + 2 = 9$$

2.
$$5 + 1 = 6$$
$$4 + 2 = 5$$
$$5 + 2 = 7$$
$$8 + 2 = 11$$

3.
$$6 + 1 = 7$$
$$9 + 2 = 11$$
$$7 + 1 = 9$$
$$4 + 1 = 5$$

4. Color the graph to show the data.

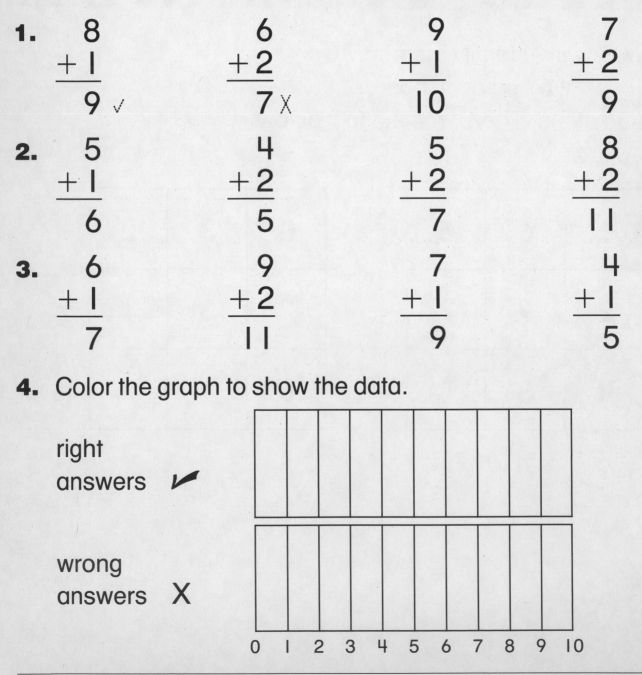

right answers ✔

wrong answers X

0 1 2 3 4 5 6 7 8 9 10

Name _____

At the Fair

6 tickets	3 tickets	4 tickets
2 tickets	7 tickets	5 tickets

Guess and check.
Ring your answers.

1. Tammy went on 3 different rides.
She used 11 tickets.
What rides could she have gone on?

2. Craig went on 3 different rides.
He used 12 tickets.
What rides could he have gone on?

Name _____

Greater, Greatest

Ring the fact that has the greater sum.
Find the sums to check.

1. 2   (2) **2.** 3   3   **3.** 4   4
     +1   (+2)   +3 +2   +5 +4

4. 1   1   **5.** 5   6   **6.** 5   5
     +1 +2   +6 +6   +5 +6

Ring the fact that has the greatest sum.
Find the sums to check.

7. 3   3   3   **8.** 6   6   5
     +2 +3 +1   +6 +7 +6

9. 2   2   2   **10.** 3   4   4
     +3 +1 +2   +3 +3 +4

11. 5   5   5   **12.** 2   1   0
      +4 +6 +5   +1 +1 +1

Use with text pages 111–112.

Name _____

Adding 1 or 2

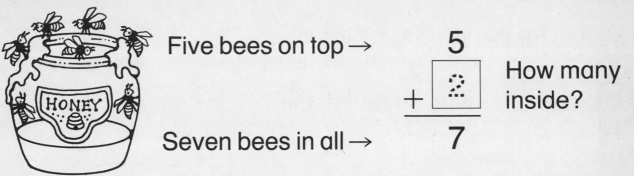

Five bees on top →

Seven bees in all →

5
+ [2] How many inside?
7

___

What number was added — 1 or 2?
Guess. Use counters to check.

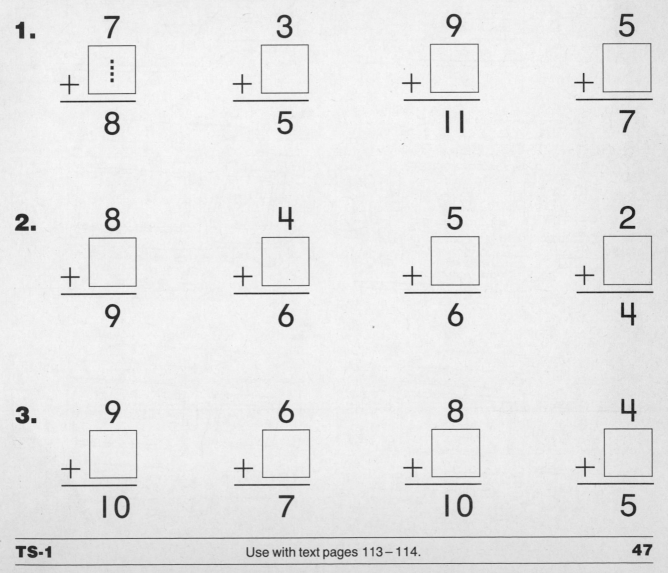

1.

7
+ [:]
8

3
+ [ ]
5

9
+ [ ]
11

5
+ [ ]
7

2.

8
+ [ ]
9

4
+ [ ]
6

5
+ [ ]
6

2
+ [ ]
4

3.

9
+ [ ]
10

6
+ [ ]
7

8
+ [ ]
10

4
+ [ ]
5

Name _____

Math Machine

The rule for the Math Machine is
<u>add 1</u>, <u>add 2</u>, or <u>add 3</u>.
Write the number to show the rule.

1.

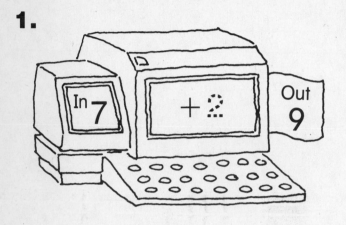

In 7 + 2 Out 9

2.

In 8 + Out 9

3.

In 8 + Out 11

4.

In 5 + Out 8

5.

In 8 + Out 10

6.

In 9 + Out 12

Name _____

Secret Numbers

Find the secret numbers.
Use the numbers on
the board.

1. Add 5 to me.
You will get 8.
Who am I?

_____

2. Add 4 to me.
Then add 1 more.
You will get 11.
Who am I?

_____

3. Add me to myself.
Then add 2 more.
You will get 12.
Who am I?

_____

4. Add 2 to me.
Then add 1 more.
You will get 12.
Who am I?

_____

5. Add 3 to me.
Then take away 1.
You will get 9.
Who am I?

_____

6. Add me to myself.
Then add 3 more.
You will get 11.
Who am I?

_____

Name _____

Is It a Double?

Complete the additions. Use doubles or doubles plus one.

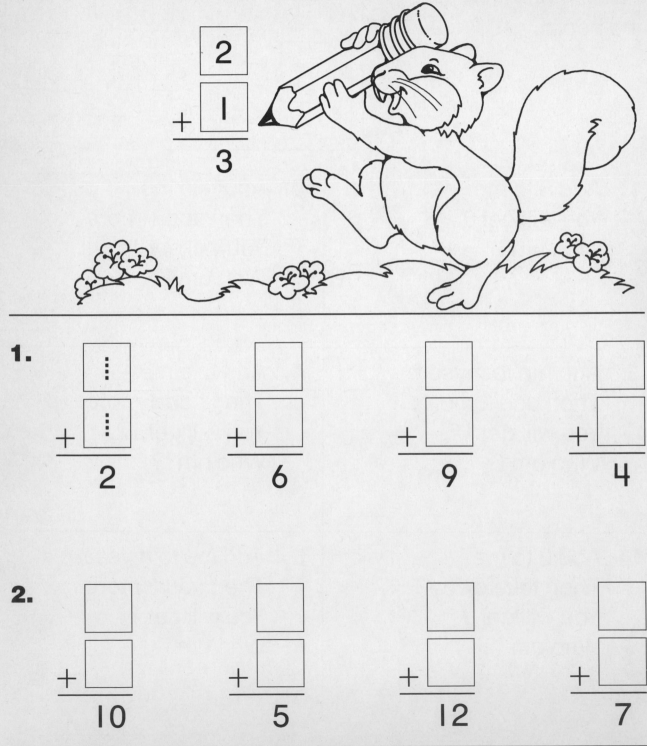

```
  2
+ 1
―――
  3
```

1.

```
  ⋮        □        □        □
+ ⋮      + □      + □      + □
―――      ―――      ―――      ―――
  2        6        9        4
```

2.

```
  □        □        □        □
+ □      + □      + □      + □
―――      ―――      ―――      ―――
 10        5       12        7
```

Name _____

Bugs For Sale

How much money in all?

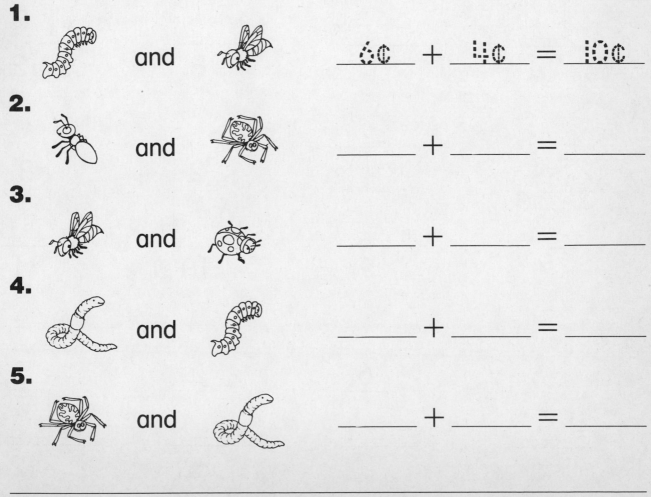

1. and   ___6¢___ + ___4¢___ = ___10¢___

2. and   ___ + ___ = ___

3. and   ___ + ___ = ___

4. and   ___ + ___ = ___

5. and   ___ + ___ = ___

Name _____

Missing Numbers

Write the missing number. Use counters to check.

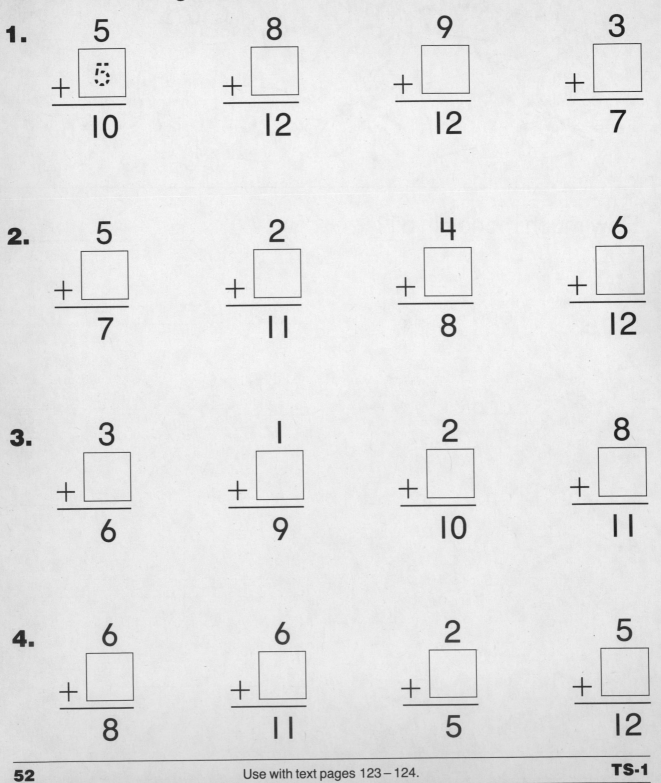

1.

5	8	9	3
+ 5	+ ☐	+ ☐	+ ☐
10	12	12	7

2.

5	2	4	6
+ ☐	+ ☐	+ ☐	+ ☐
7	11	8	12

3.

3	1	2	8
+ ☐	+ ☐	+ ☐	+ ☐
6	9	10	11

4.

6	6	2	5
+ ☐	+ ☐	+ ☐	+ ☐
8	11	5	12

Addison-Wesley | All Rights Reserved

Name _____

What Is Missing?

Add the first two numbers.
Write the first sum on the line.
Then find the missing number.

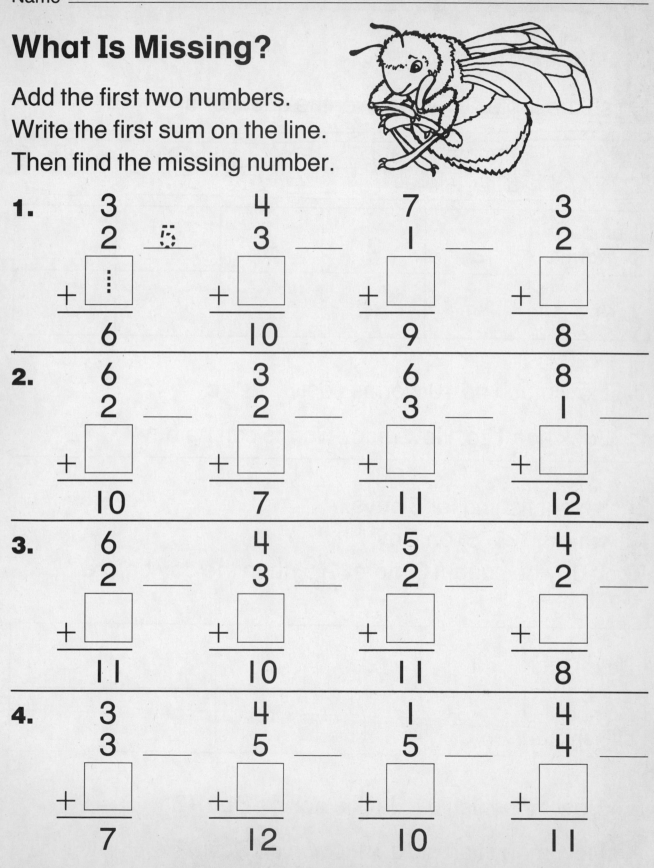

1.

3	5	4	__	7	__	3	__
2		3		1		2	
+ [ ]		+ [ ]		+ [ ]		+ [ ]	
6		10		9		8	

2.

6	__	3	__	6	__	8	__
2		2		3		1	
+ [ ]		+ [ ]		+ [ ]		+ [ ]	
10		7		11		12	

3.

6	__	4	__	5	__	4	__
2		3		2		2	
+ [ ]		+ [ ]		+ [ ]		+ [ ]	
11		10		11		8	

4.

3	__	4	__	1	__	4	__
3		5		5		4	
+ [ ]		+ [ ]		+ [ ]		+ [ ]	
7		12		10		11	

Name _____

Gone Fishing

Finish the table. Then answer the questions.

Worm Bait - 2 🪱 for 3¢

Number of Worms	2	4	6	___	___
Cost	3¢	6¢	___	___	___

1. How much do 10 worms cost? ____ ¢

2. Jack has 12¢. How many worms can he buy? ____

Jack went fishing for 5 days.
He caught 1 🐟 on Day 1.
Each day he caught 3 more 🐟 than the day before.

Day	1	2	3	___	___
Number of Fish	1	4	7	___	___

3. How many fish did Jack catch on Day 4? ____

4. How many fish did Jack catch on Day 5? ____

Name _____

Guess and Check

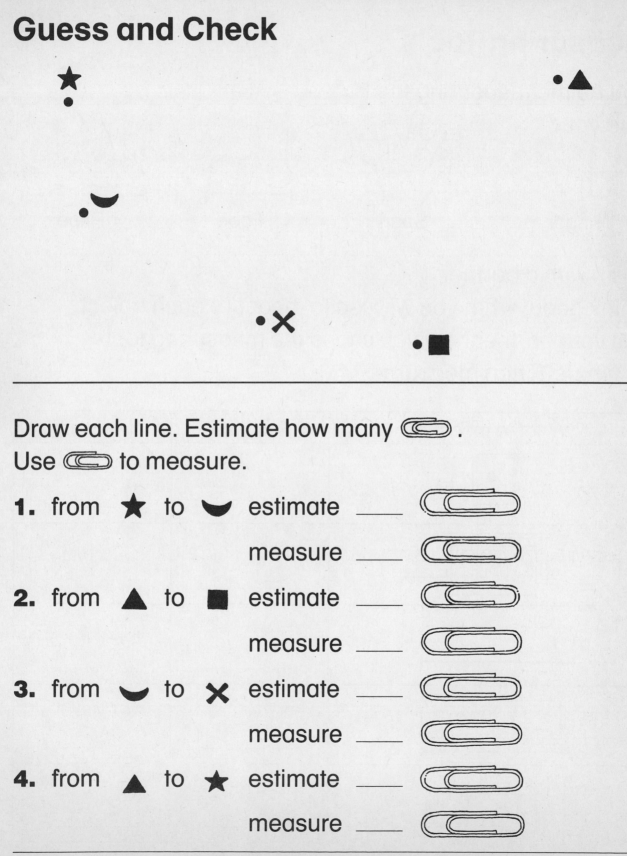

Draw each line. Estimate how many ⬭.
Use ⬭ to measure.

1. from ★ to ⌣ estimate ____ ⬭

measure ____ ⬭

2. from ▲ to ■ estimate ____ ⬭

measure ____ ⬭

3. from ⌣ to ✗ estimate ____ ⬭

measure ____ ⬭

4. from ▲ to ★ estimate ____ ⬭

measure ____ ⬭

Name _____

Measuring Tools

You be the measuring tool!
Use your

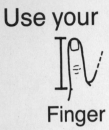

Finger

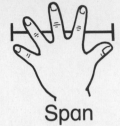

Span

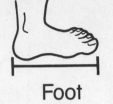

Foot

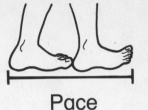

Pace

Work with a partner.

Think about what you will use to measure each object.

Tell your partner how you chose the measuring tool.

Estimate. Then measure.

What to measure	Estimate	Measure
	_____	_____
	_____	_____
	_____	_____
	_____	_____
	_____	_____

Name _____

Measurement Hunt

Go on a measurement hunt in your classroom.

1. Find something longer than this line.

_____

Draw it here.

Measure it. _____ inches

2. Find something shorter than this line.

_____

Draw it here.

Measure it. _____ inches

3. Find something about as long as this line.

_____

Draw it here.

Measure it. _____ inches

Name _____

How Far Is It?

Dear Family,
In our class we are learning to measure in feet. The activities on this page involve standard units of measure (feet) and nonstandard units (shoes). As you work along with your child, he or she will begin to understand the importance of using standard units of measure.

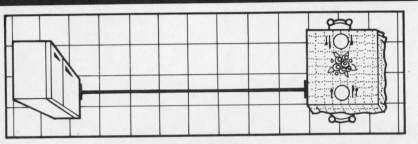

Work with a family member. Measure each distance 3 times. Use your 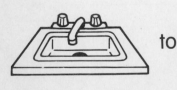. Use a family member's . Use a ▭ .

to _____ your shoe
_____ family member's shoe
_____ foot ruler

to _____ your shoe
_____ family member's shoe
_____ foot ruler

Talk about it.
Are your measures the same?
Is a 👟 a good way to measure?
Tell why or why not.

Name _____

String Measures

Work with 3 friends.
You need 🧶 and ✂.
Cut pieces of string to measure each student's

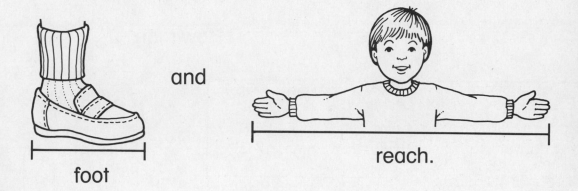

foot   and   reach.

Compare your measurements.

Whose foot is shortest?   _____

Whose foot is longest?   _____

Whose foot is in between?   _____

_____

Whose reach is shortest?   _____

Whose reach is longest?   _____

Whose reach is in between?   _____

Name _____

Block Busters

Guess how many blocks will cover the shape.
Use pattern blocks.
Cover the shape with blocks to check.

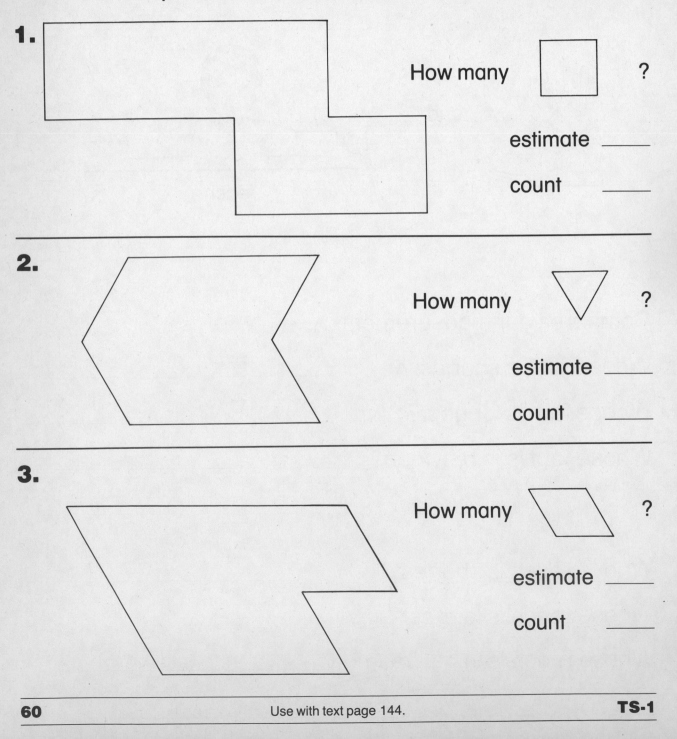

1.

How many ☐ ?

estimate _____

count _____

2.

How many ▽ ?

estimate _____

count _____

3.

How many ▱ ?

estimate _____

count _____

Name _____

Distances Around Shapes

How far is it around each one?
Use your 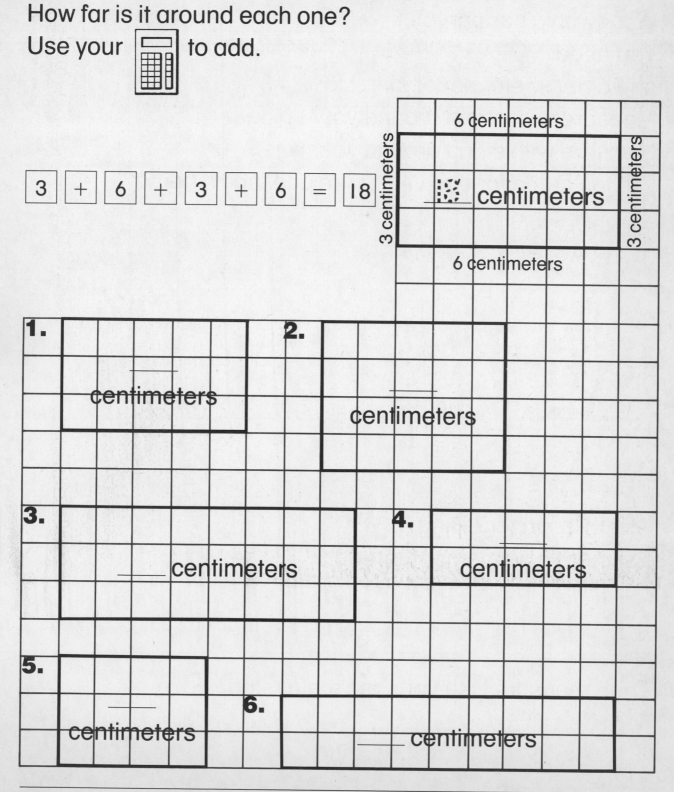 to add.

$$3 + 6 + 3 + 6 = 18$$

6 centimeters

3 centimeters

18 centimeters

3 centimeters

6 centimeters

1. _____ centimeters

2. _____ centimeters

3. _____ centimeters

4. _____ centimeters

5. _____ centimeters

6. _____ centimeters

Name _____

Strings and Strips

Work with a partner.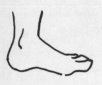
You need ⬤ , ✂ ,
and a decimeter paper strip.

Measure with string around your ankle.

Measure with string around your wrist.

Cut the string for each measure and tape it here.

Which is longer? Ring it.

Estimate how many decimeters.

_____   _____

Then measure with your decimeter strip.

_____   _____

Name _____

Scavenger Hunt

Work in groups of 3. Take turns.
- Find the pictured object.
- Find an object that feels lighter.
- Find an object that feels heavier.

Then draw the objects.

Lighter		Heavier

1.

2.

3.

Addison-Wesley | All Rights Reserved

Name _____

Match Ups

Use number cards 1 – 8.
Make an estimate for each picture.
Use each number only once.
Put the number cards on the pictures.
Make sure all of your estimates make sense.
Then write your answers.

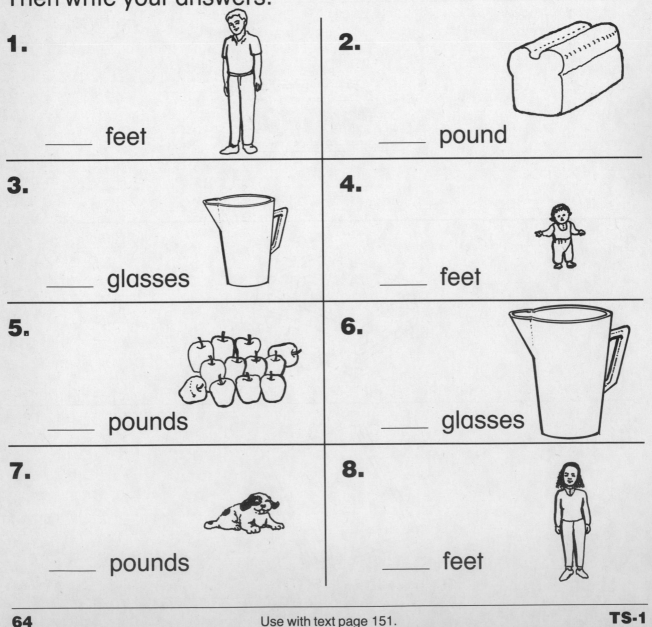

1. ____ feet

2. ____ pound

3. ____ glasses

4. ____ feet

5. ____ pounds

6. ____ glasses

7. ____ pounds

8. ____ feet

Balloon Facts

Color the balloon with the smaller difference.
Tell how you know.

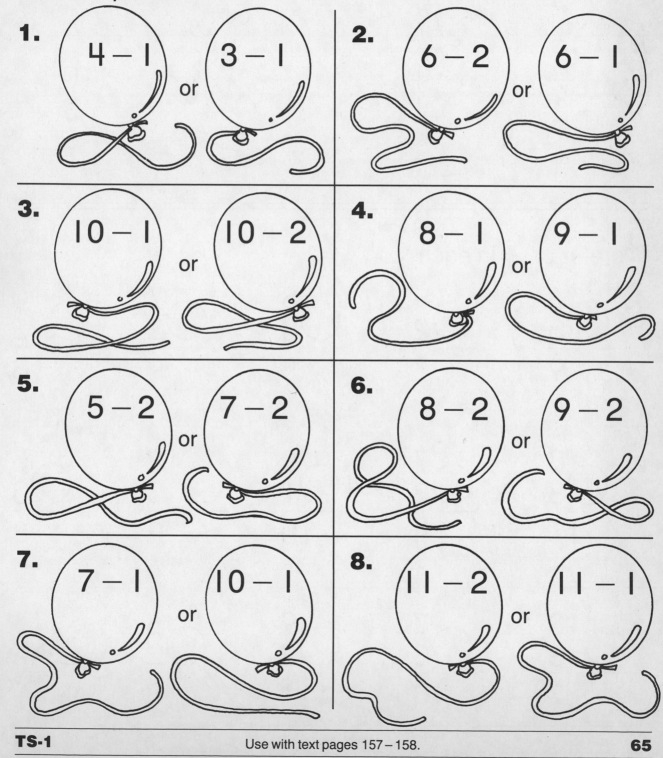

1. 4 – 1 or 3 – 1

2. 6 – 2 or 6 – 1

3. 10 – 1 or 10 – 2

4. 8 – 1 or 9 – 1

5. 5 – 2 or 7 – 2

6. 8 – 2 or 9 – 2

7. 7 – 1 or 10 – 1

8. 11 – 2 or 11 – 1

Name _____

Add or Subtract

Add.
+

Subtract.
−

$$\begin{array}{r} 9 \\ +2 \\ \hline 11 \end{array}$$

$$\begin{array}{r} 10 \\ -3 \\ \hline 7 \end{array}$$

Write + or − in each ◯.

1.
$$\begin{array}{r} \oplus\ 6 \\ 3 \\ \hline 9 \end{array}$$
$$\begin{array}{r} \ominus\ 9 \\ 2 \\ \hline 7 \end{array}$$
$$\begin{array}{r} \bigcirc\ 8 \\ 3 \\ \hline 5 \end{array}$$
$$\begin{array}{r} \bigcirc\ 7 \\ 2 \\ \hline 9 \end{array}$$
$$\begin{array}{r} \bigcirc\ 10 \\ 2 \\ \hline 8 \end{array}$$

2.
$$\begin{array}{r} \bigcirc\ 8 \\ 3 \\ \hline 11 \end{array}$$
$$\begin{array}{r} \bigcirc\ 7 \\ 3 \\ \hline 4 \end{array}$$
$$\begin{array}{r} \bigcirc\ 9 \\ 1 \\ \hline 10 \end{array}$$
$$\begin{array}{r} \bigcirc\ 12 \\ 3 \\ \hline 9 \end{array}$$
$$\begin{array}{r} \bigcirc\ 5 \\ 3 \\ \hline 8 \end{array}$$

3.
$$\begin{array}{r} \bigcirc\ 10 \\ 3 \\ \hline 7 \end{array}$$
$$\begin{array}{r} \bigcirc\ 7 \\ 3 \\ \hline 10 \end{array}$$
$$\begin{array}{r} \bigcirc\ 9 \\ 2 \\ \hline 11 \end{array}$$
$$\begin{array}{r} \bigcirc\ 6 \\ 2 \\ \hline 8 \end{array}$$
$$\begin{array}{r} \bigcirc\ 11 \\ 2 \\ \hline 9 \end{array}$$

Name _____

Missing Data

The rule for the Math Machine is
<u>subtract 1</u>, <u>subtract 2</u>, or <u>subtract 3</u>.
Write the number to show the rule.

1. 9 − ⋮ 8

2. 11 − 8

3. 8 − 6

4. 10 − 7

5. 10 − 8

6. 12 − 9

Name _____

Guess the Answer

Read each problem.

Will the answer be more or less than

the number in the ☐?

Ring your guess. Calculate the answer to check.

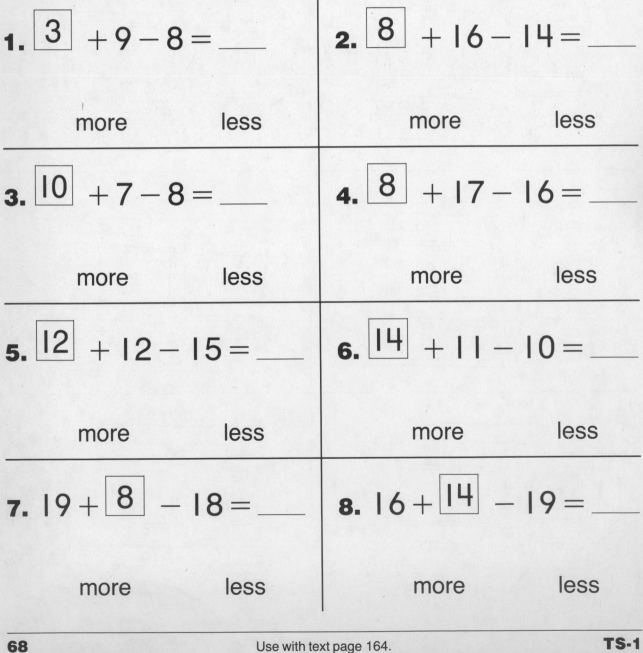

1. $\boxed{3} + 9 - 8 = \underline{\quad}$

         more   less

2. $\boxed{8} + 16 - 14 = \underline{\quad}$

         more   less

3. $\boxed{10} + 7 - 8 = \underline{\quad}$

         more   less

4. $\boxed{8} + 17 - 16 = \underline{\quad}$

         more   less

5. $\boxed{12} + 12 - 15 = \underline{\quad}$

         more   less

6. $\boxed{14} + 11 - 10 = \underline{\quad}$

         more   less

7. $19 + \boxed{8} - 18 = \underline{\quad}$

         more   less

8. $16 + \boxed{14} - 19 = \underline{\quad}$

         more   less

Name _____

Use the Clues

Look at the pictures.
Read each question.
Write how many went away.

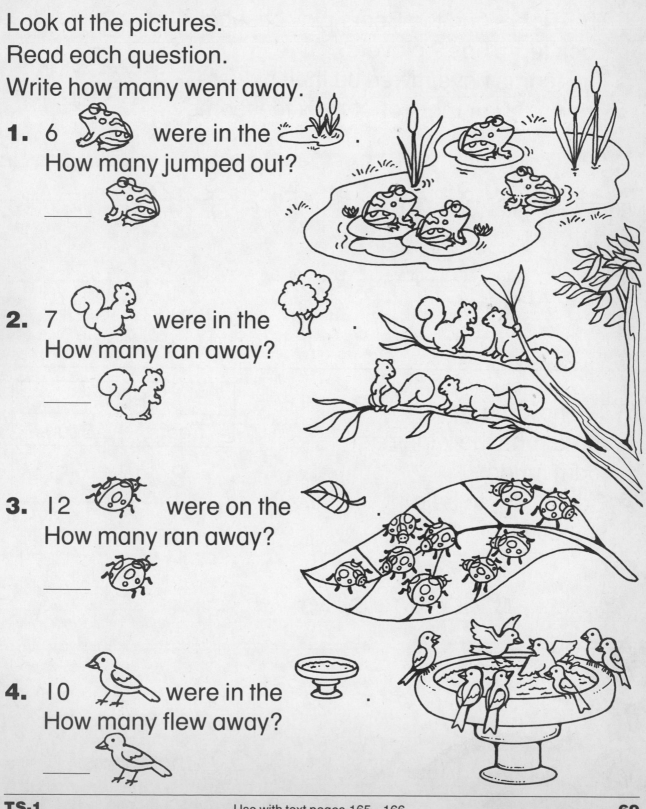

1. 6 were in the .
How many jumped out?

____

2. 7 were in the
How many ran away?

____

3. 12 were on the
How many ran away?

____

4. 10 were in the .
How many flew away?

Name _____

Logic

1. The Tigers and the Bears play baseball.
Each team has 9 players.
The teams have mixed up their players.
Draw ⚲ or mark an X to fix the teams.

Tigers ⚲ ⚲ ⚲ ⚲ ⚲ ⚲ ⚲ ⚲ ⚲ ⚲ ⚲

Bears ⚲ ⚲ ⚲ ⚲ ⚲ ⚲ ⚲

---

2. Tell how many
more runs the winning
team made.
Color ⚾ to help
you count.

Runs	
Tigers	Bears
8	5

Tigers ⚾ ⚾ ⚾ ⚾ ⚾ ⚾ ⚾ ⚾

Bears ⚾ ⚾ ⚾ ⚾ ⚾ ⚾ ⚾ ⚾

_____ more runs

Name _____

Pairs of Sentences

Think about each pair.
Ring the one that has the greater answer.

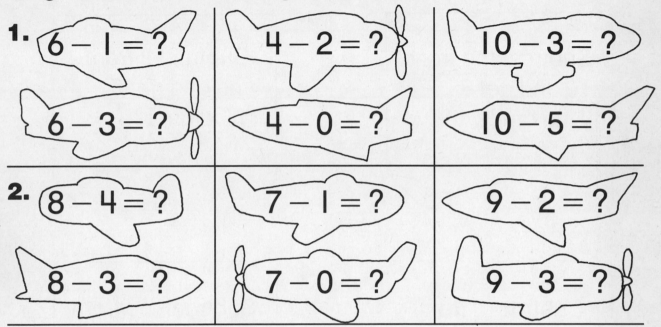

1.
6 − 1 = ?   4 − 2 = ?   10 − 3 = ?
6 − 3 = ?   4 − 0 = ?   10 − 5 = ?

2.
8 − 4 = ?   7 − 1 = ?   9 − 2 = ?
8 − 3 = ?   7 − 0 = ?   9 − 3 = ?

Ring the one that has the smaller answer.

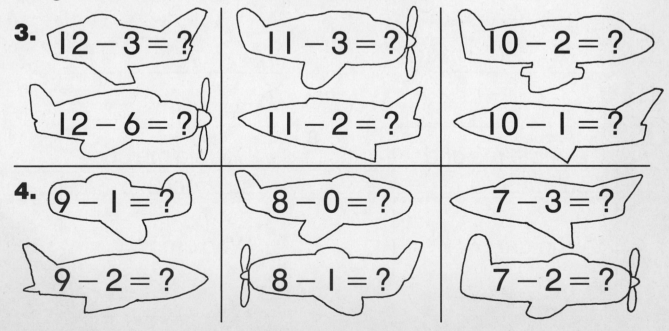

3.
12 − 3 = ?   11 − 3 = ?   10 − 2 = ?
12 − 6 = ?   11 − 2 = ?   10 − 1 = ?

4.
9 − 1 = ?   8 − 0 = ?   7 − 3 = ?
9 − 2 = ?   8 − 1 = ?   7 − 2 = ?

Name _____

Number Riddles

Read the riddle.
Write a number to answer the question.

1.

Subtract me from
10 and get 8.
Who am I?

_____

2.

Subtract 2 from
me and get 5.
Who am I?

_____

3.

Subtract 3 from
me and get 8.
Who am I?

_____

4.

Subtract me from
12 and get 9.
Who am I?

_____

5.

Double me and
subtract 1 to
get 7.
Who am I?

_____

6.

Double me and
subtract 3 to
get 7.
Who am I?

_____

Name _____

The Fruit Basket

The basket contains:

4 bananas	8 plums
7 oranges	5 red apples
11 pears	7 yellow apples

Write a number sentence and the answer.

1. How many apples are there in all?

_____

_____ apples

2. Joe ate 3 pears. How many pears were left?

_____

_____ pears

3. Mary ate all the bananas and plums. How much fruit did she eat in all?

_____

_____ in all

4. Two of the oranges were bad. How many oranges were good?

_____

_____ oranges

Name _____

Guess the Rule

Guess the rule that was used to sort the solids.
Write the letter of the rule on the line.
Use each rule only once.

Rules
A. They can be stacked one on top of another.
B. They have no sharp points.
C. They can roll.

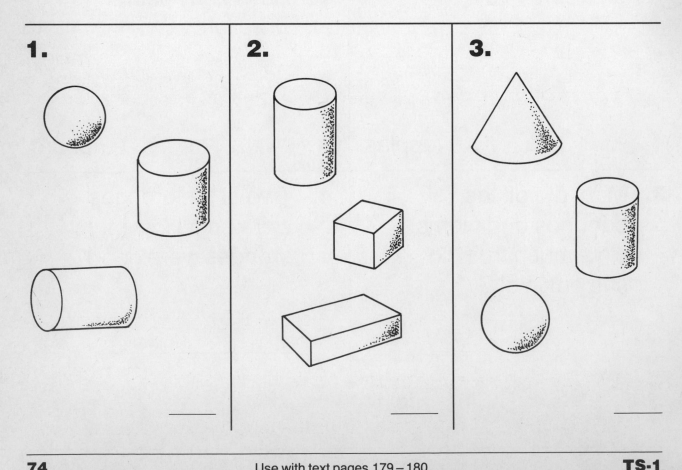

1. _____

2. _____

3. _____

Name _____

Organizing Data

Work in a group of 4.

Each student picks one of these shapes:

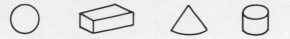

Find things with the same shape in your classroom.

Look in books for pictures, too.

---

1. Make a graph to show what you found.
Color a ☐ for each solid you found.

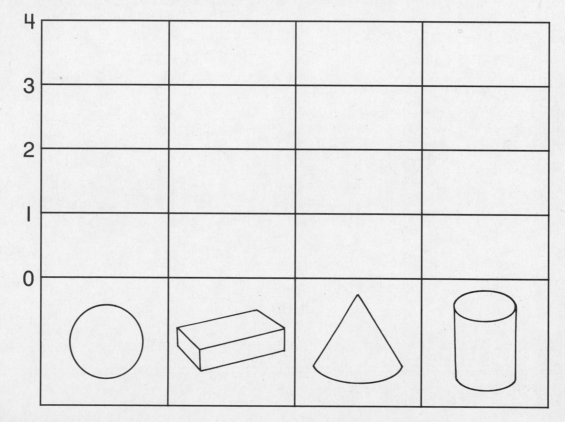

2. Which solid shape did you find the most? _____

3. Which solid shape did you find the least? _____

Name _____

Find the Treasure

Which chest has the treasure?
Look at the chests. Then read the clues.
Ring the correct chest.

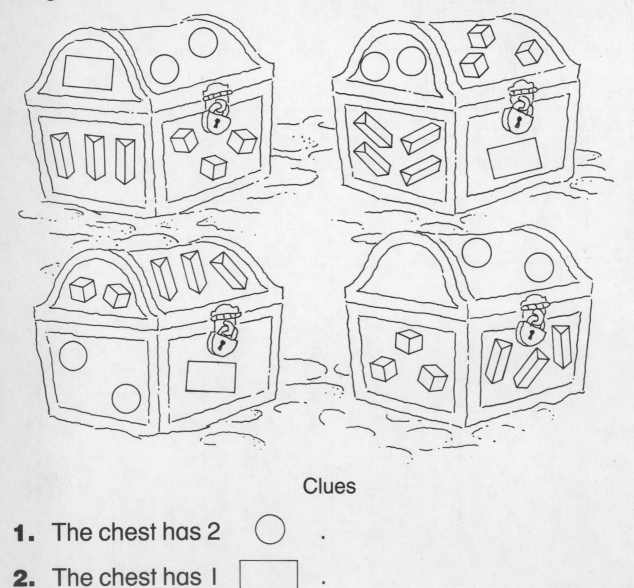

Clues

1. The chest has 2 ◯ .

2. The chest has 1 ▭ .

3. The chest has 3 ⬜ .

4. The chest has more ⬡ than ⬜ .

Name _____

Visualizing Figures

Draw each figure.
Begin with the part given.

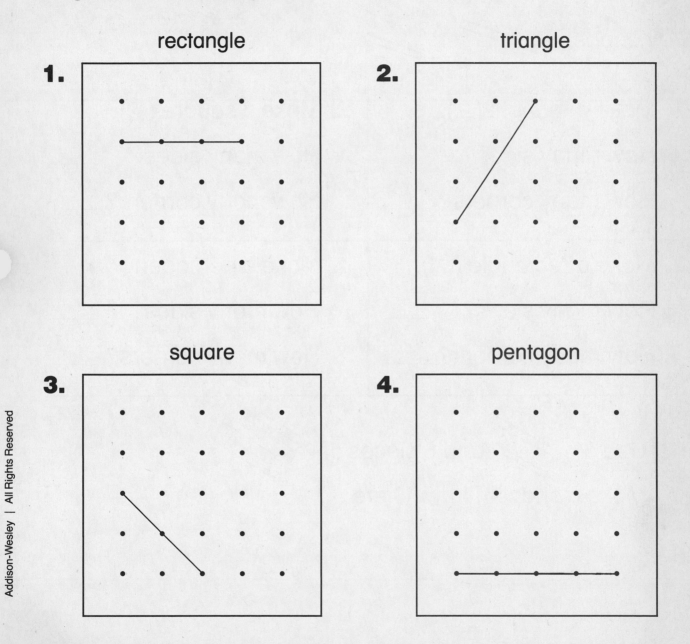

rectangle

1.

triangle

2.

square

3.

pentagon

4.

5. Compare your figures with those of a partner. Talk about how many sides and corners each figure has.

Name _____

Shape Up

Make shapes.

Use _____ and _____ .

You choose _____ or _____ .

1. Make a triangle (△).

How many sides? _____

How many corners? _____

2. Make a square (□).

How many sides? _____

How many corners? _____

3. Make a rectangle (▭).

How many sides? _____

How many corners? _____

4. Make a pentagon (⬠).

How many sides? _____

How many corners? _____

5. Use 6 _____ and 6 pieces of _____ .

Make a shape. Draw it here.

How many sides? _____

How many corners? _____

Blips and Blops

1. These are blips.

These are <u>not</u> blips.

Ring the blips. Tell how you know.

2. These are blops.

These are <u>not</u> blops.

Ring the blops. Tell how you know.

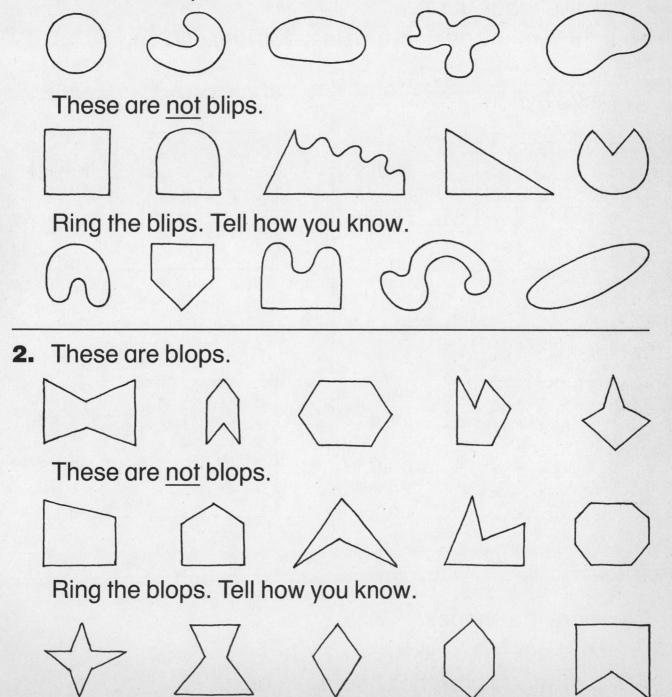

Name _____

Creating Shapes

Work in a group of 4. Use geoboards.
Each student makes a shape on 9 pegs.
Draw all shapes here.
Write how many pegs are inside, outside, and on.

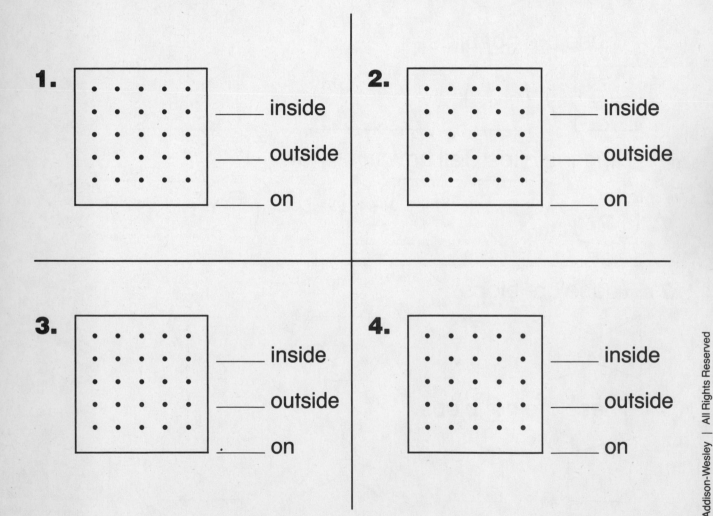

1. _____ inside

   _____ outside

   _____ on

2. _____ inside

   _____ outside

   _____ on

3. _____ inside

   _____ outside

   _____ on

4. _____ inside

   _____ outside

   _____ on

Compare the shapes.
Which shapes are alike?
Tell your group how the shapes are alike.

Name _____

Identifying Symmetric Figures

Color symmetric figures RED .
X figures that are not symmetric.
Ring to show why.

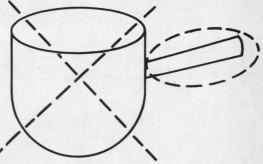

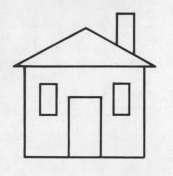

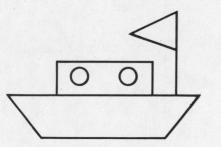

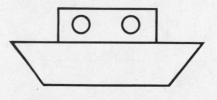

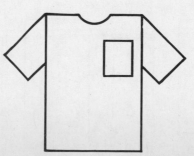

Name _____

What Comes Next?

Look at the pattern.
Color the figure that comes next.

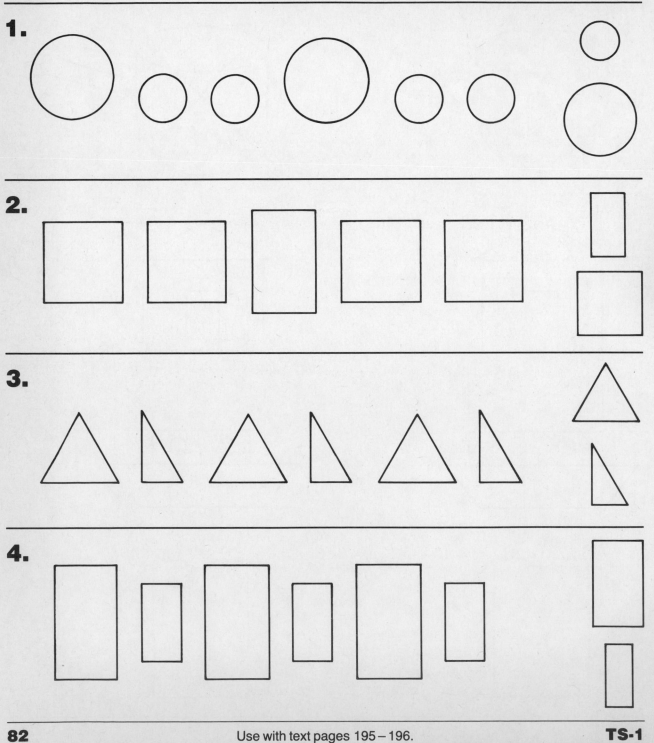

1.

2.

3.

4.

Name _____

Pattern Place

Look for a pattern.
Finish the picture.

1. Where is the chimney on this house?

2. What kind of roof does this house have?

3. How many windows does this house have?

4. What kind of door does this house have?

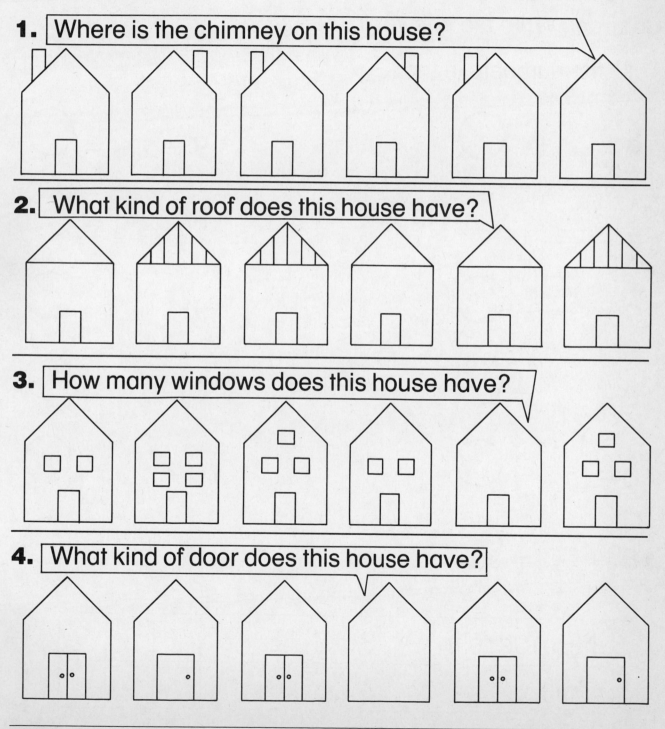

Name _____

Subtract and Tally

Throw a number cube.
Write that number in the ☐.
Subtract. Write the answer in the ○.

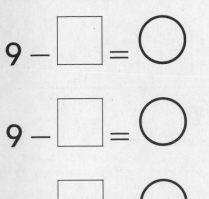

Tally the numbers in the ○.

$9 - \boxed{} = \bigcirc$ $9 - \boxed{} = \bigcirc$

$9 - \boxed{} = \bigcirc$ $9 - \boxed{} = \bigcirc$

$9 - \boxed{} = \bigcirc$ $9 - \boxed{} = \bigcirc$

$10 - \boxed{} = \bigcirc$ $10 - \boxed{} = \bigcirc$

$10 - \boxed{} = \bigcirc$ $10 - \boxed{} = \bigcirc$

$10 - \boxed{} = \bigcirc$ $10 - \boxed{} = \bigcirc$

Numbers in ○	3	4	5	6	7	8	9
Tallies							

Name _____

Finding and Describing Patterns

Subtract.
Write two more facts to continue the patterns.

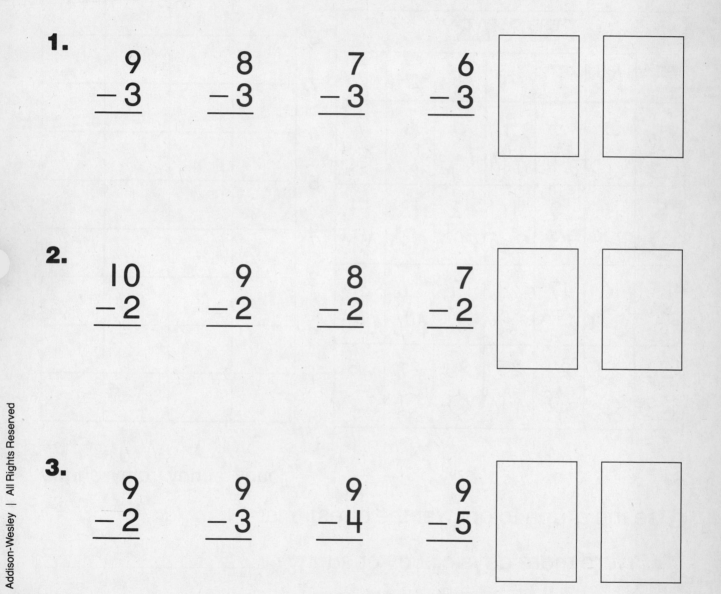

1.

$$\begin{array}{r} 9 \\ -3 \\ \hline \end{array} \qquad \begin{array}{r} 8 \\ -3 \\ \hline \end{array} \qquad \begin{array}{r} 7 \\ -3 \\ \hline \end{array} \qquad \begin{array}{r} 6 \\ -3 \\ \hline \end{array}$$

2.

$$\begin{array}{r} 10 \\ -2 \\ \hline \end{array} \qquad \begin{array}{r} 9 \\ -2 \\ \hline \end{array} \qquad \begin{array}{r} 8 \\ -2 \\ \hline \end{array} \qquad \begin{array}{r} 7 \\ -2 \\ \hline \end{array}$$

3.

$$\begin{array}{r} 9 \\ -2 \\ \hline \end{array} \qquad \begin{array}{r} 9 \\ -3 \\ \hline \end{array} \qquad \begin{array}{r} 9 \\ -4 \\ \hline \end{array} \qquad \begin{array}{r} 9 \\ -5 \\ \hline \end{array}$$

4. Work with a partner. Take turns.
Describe the patterns.

Name _____

Weather Ways

Color squares on the graph to match the data
on the weather calendar.

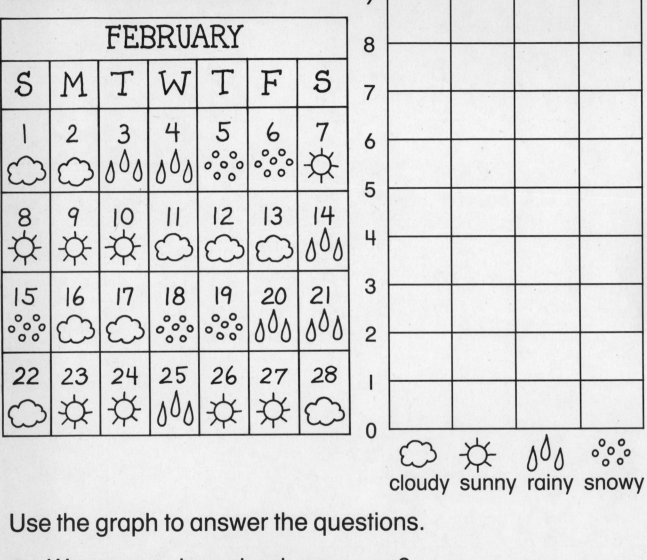

Use the graph to answer the questions.

1. Were more days cloudy or sunny? _____

2. On how many days did it snow? _____

3. How many more days were sunny than rainy? _____

4. How many more days were cloudy than snowy? _____

Name _____

What Was It?

Use a to help you find what number was subtracted.

Can you find an easy way to solve?

1. $8 - \boxed{2} = 6$ $9 - \boxed{} = 5$

2. $10 - \boxed{} = 4$ $9 - \boxed{} = 6$

3. $10 - \boxed{} = 2$ $10 - \boxed{} = 8$

4. $7 - \boxed{} = 5$ $9 - \boxed{} = 5$

5. $10 - \boxed{} = 5$ $8 - \boxed{} = 3$

Name _____

Reading a Graph

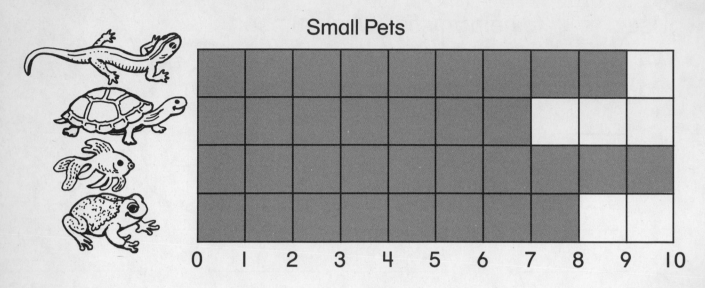

Small Pets

0 1 2 3 4 5 6 7 8 9 10

Write subtraction facts.
Use the graph to help you.

1. How many more [frog] than [turtle] ?

___ – ___ = ___

2. How many fewer [turtle] than [lizard] ?

___ – ___ = ___

3. How many more [fish] than [frog] ?

___ – ___ = ___

Name _____

Sentence Search

Ring three numbers in a row that can make a subtraction sentence.

Hint:
There are 10 in all.

(12   5   7)   8   9   4   5

3   7   5   10   6   4   1

6   11   4   7   2   8   3

10   2   8   5   12   3   9

7   9   6   3   10   7   3

12   4   8   7   11   2   9

Name _____

Which One Tells?

Ring the number sentence that tells what
is happening.
Write the answer.

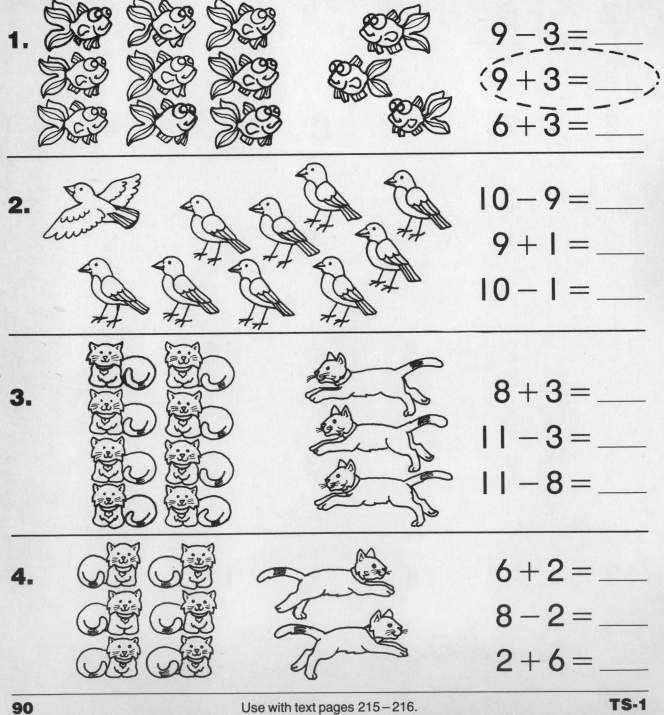

1.
9 − 3 = ____
9 + 3 = ____
6 + 3 = ____

2.
10 − 9 = ____
9 + 1 = ____
10 − 1 = ____

3.
8 + 3 = ____
11 − 3 = ____
11 − 8 = ____

4.
6 + 2 = ____
8 − 2 = ____
2 + 6 = ____

Name _____

Using Subtraction Strategies

Dear Family,
 Our class has been learning strategies that help us to subtract. As your child works through the path, ask him or her to explain which fact strategy he or she used.

Help 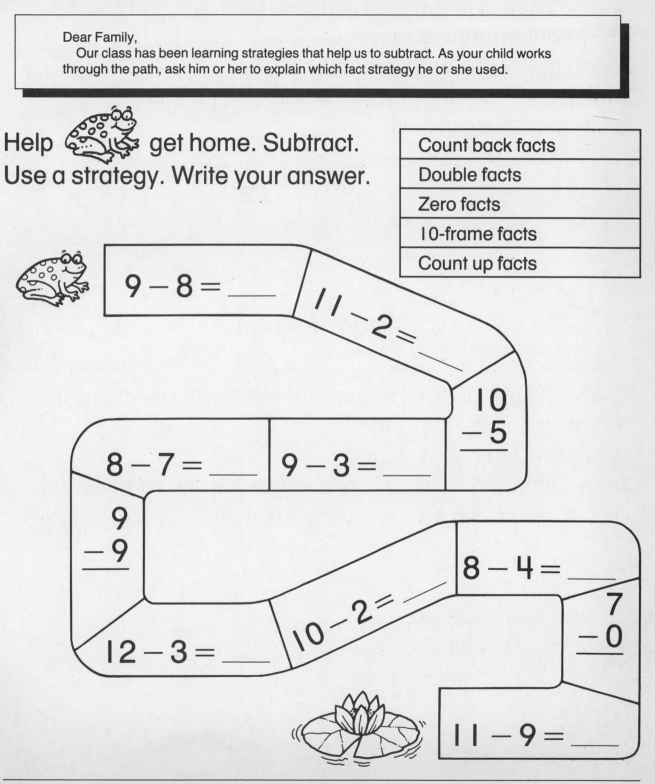 get home. Subtract.
Use a strategy. Write your answer.

| Count back facts |
| Double facts |
| Zero facts |
| 10-frame facts |
| Count up facts |

$9 - 8 =$ _____

$11 - 2 =$ _____

$\begin{array}{r} 10 \\ -\ 5 \\ \hline \end{array}$

$8 - 7 =$ _____

$9 - 3 =$ _____

$\begin{array}{r} 9 \\ -\ 9 \\ \hline \end{array}$

$8 - 4 =$ _____

$12 - 3 =$ _____

$10 - 2 =$ _____

$\begin{array}{r} 7 \\ -\ 0 \\ \hline \end{array}$

$11 - 9 =$ _____

Name _____

Which One?

The 5 children in the Brown family each got a present.
Mary got something to wear.
Jason got something to ride.
Tim and Jim got things to play with.
What did Sara get? Ring it.

The 4 children in the Harper family each chose a shape.
Rachel's shape is round.
Mark's shape has 3 sides.
Josh's shape has 4 corners and 4 sides the same length.
Which shape did Maria choose? Ring it.

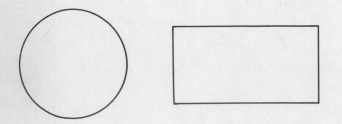 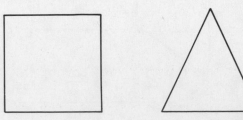

Name _____

One More Ten

Work in a group.
Take a pile of paper clips.
Make 8 trains of 10 clips.
Take 9 extra clips.
Show the set. Write the number.
Write the number that has 1 more ten.

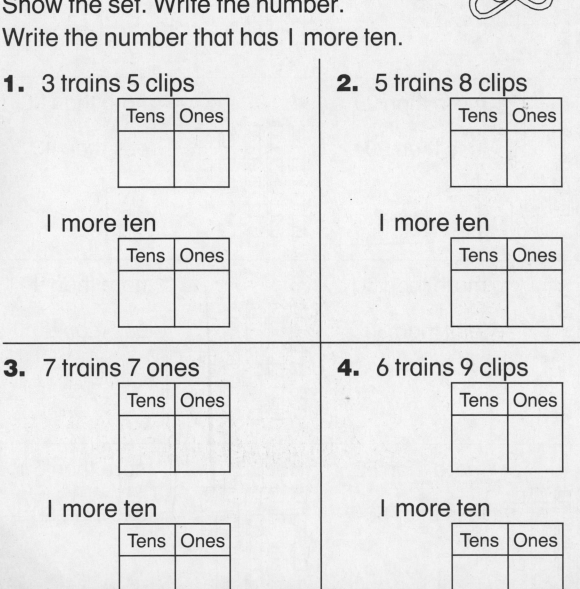

1. 3 trains 5 clips

Tens	Ones

1 more ten

Tens	Ones

2. 5 trains 8 clips

Tens	Ones

1 more ten

Tens	Ones

3. 7 trains 7 ones

Tens	Ones

1 more ten

Tens	Ones

4. 6 trains 9 clips

Tens	Ones

1 more ten

Tens	Ones

Name _____

More or Less?

Ring the better estimate. Then count and write how many.

1. more than 40

(less than 40)

35

2. more than 40

less than 40

3. more than 20

less than 20

4. more than 40

less than 40

5. more than 30

less than 30

6. more than 40

less than 40

7. more than 50

less than 50

8. more than 60

less than 60

Name _____

Scrambled Words

Unscramble the decade names.
Write the words. Then match to the number.

1. fityf

2. ent

3. ytorf

4. gheity

5. tynewt

6. tryith

7. xsiyt

8. netyin

9. vesenty

10

20

30

40

50

60

70

80

90

Name _____

Stringing Tens

Put 10 beads on a string.
Fill as many strings as you can.

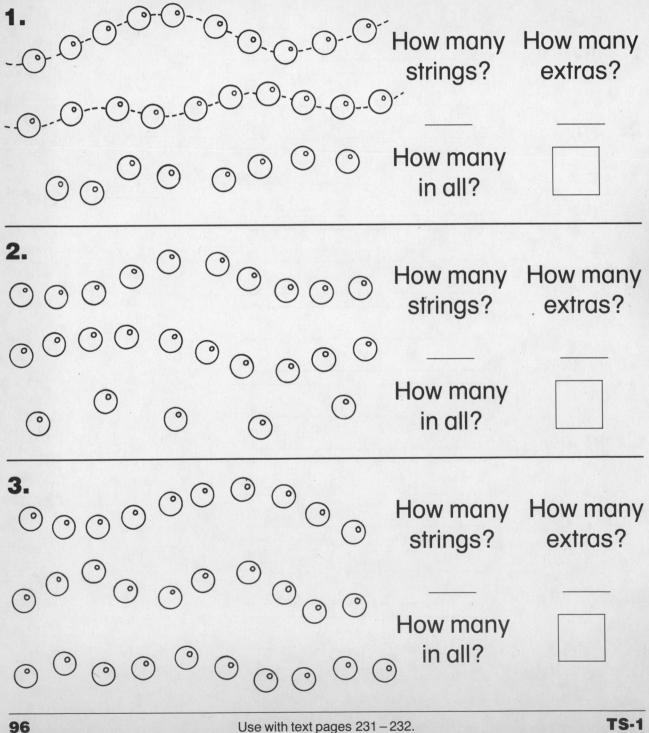

1.

How many
strings?

How many
extras?

_____

How many
in all?

2.

How many
strings?

How many
extras?

_____

How many
in all?

3.

How many
strings?

How many
extras?

_____

How many
in all?

Name _____

Count the Models

Write how many.

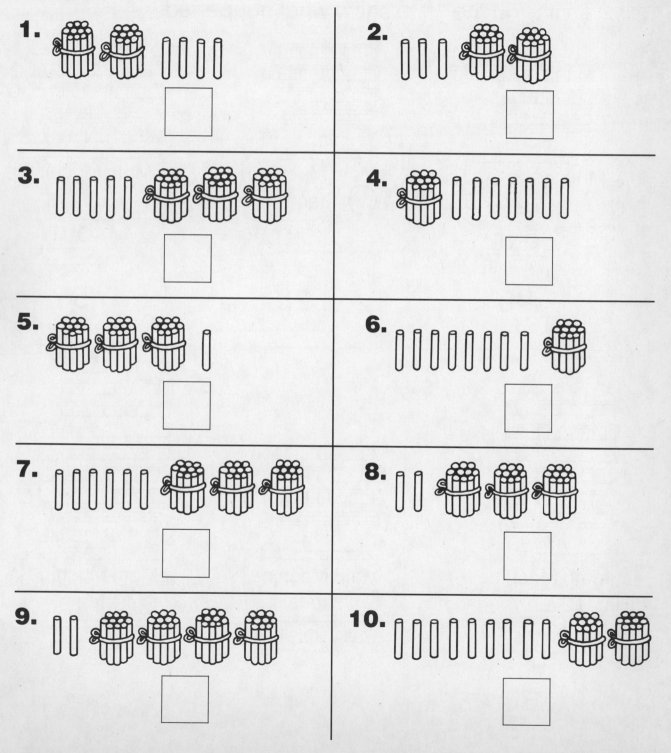

1.

2.

3.

4.

5.

6.

7.

8.

9.

10.

Name _____

Math Machine

The Math Machine adds and subtracts tens.
Write + or − in the ○ to show what happened.

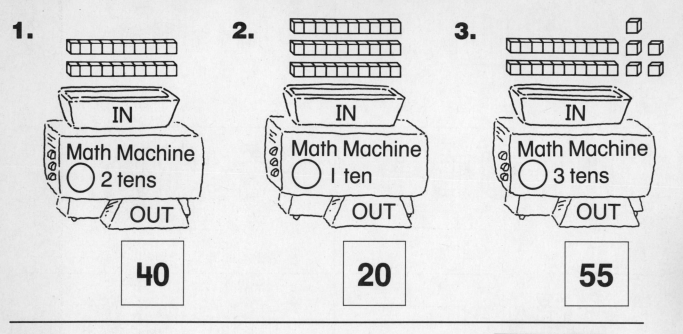

1.

Math Machine
○ 2 tens

40

2.

Math Machine
○ 1 ten

20

3.

Math Machine
○ 3 tens

55

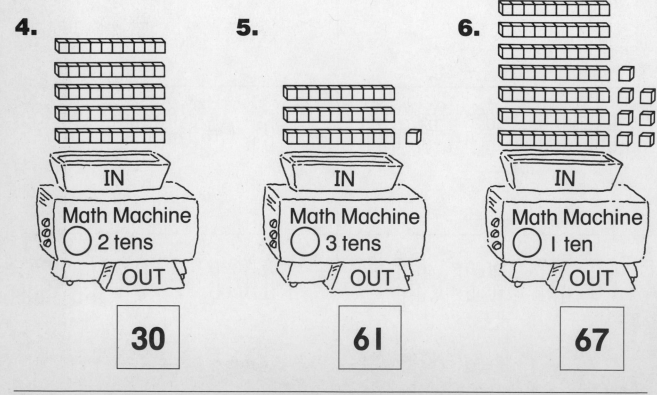

4.

Math Machine
○ 2 tens

30

5.

Math Machine
○ 3 tens

61

6.

Math Machine
○ 1 ten

67

Name _____

Different Amounts

Use your punchout pennies and dimes.
Write to show the coins I could have. Write the amounts.

Name _____

Spending Money

Buy the gift.
How much do you have left?

1.

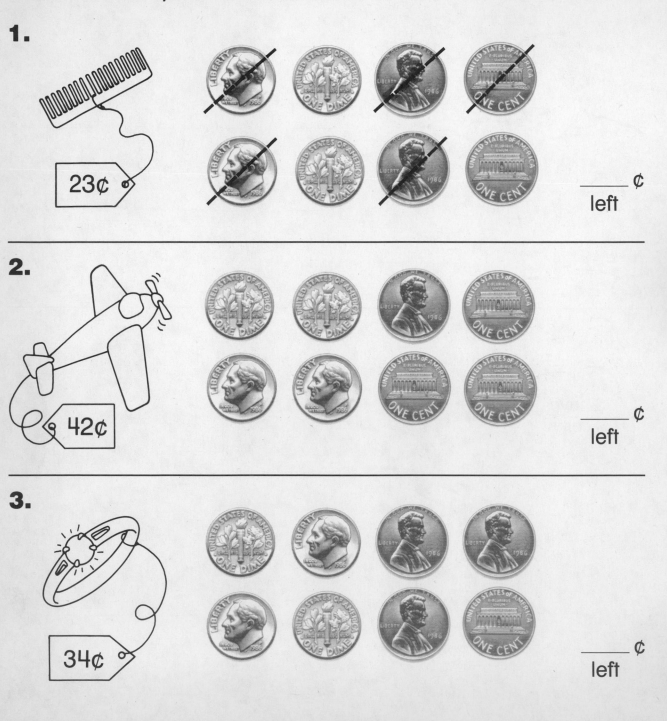

23¢

_____ ¢
left

2.

42¢

_____ ¢
left

3.

34¢

_____ ¢
left

Use with text pages 239–240.

TS-1

Name _____

How Much Money?

How much money is there?
Ring the answer that makes sense.
Use punchout coins to check.

1. 3 dimes
same number of pennies

    30¢   33¢

2. 2 dimes
1 more penny than dimes

    23¢   32¢

3. 5 dimes
1 less penny than
dimes

    54¢   56¢

4. 3 dimes
2 less pennies than
dimes

    35¢   31¢

5. 1 penny
4 more dimes than
pennies

    11¢   51¢

6. 5 pennies
1 less dime than
pennies

    65¢   45¢

7. 6 dimes
2 more pennies than
dimes

    64¢   68¢

8. 3 pennies
1 less dime than
pennies

    33¢   23¢

Name _____

Parts of Number Charts

1	2	3	4	5	6	7	8	9	10
11	12	13	14	15	16	17	18	19	20
21	22	23	24	25	26	27	28	29	30
31	32	33	34	35	36	37	38	39	40
41	42	43	44	45	46	47	48	49	50

Use the chart. Write the missing numbers in these parts of the chart.

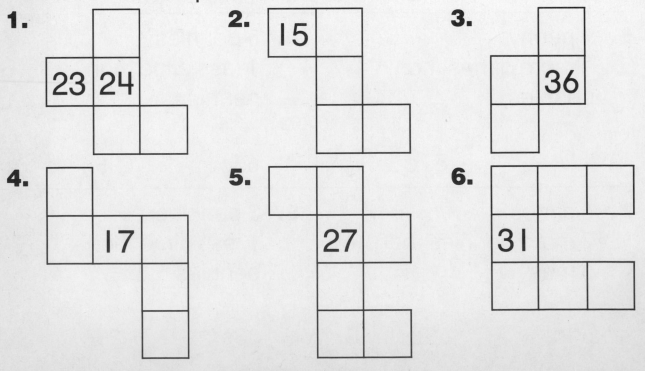

1.

23 | 24

2.

15

3.

36

4.

17

5.

27

6.

31

Name _____

Matching Order

Look at the order of the shapes in the box.

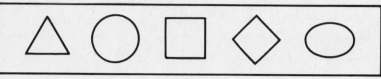

Write the number and draw the shapes below so the numbers are in order.
Do the shapes follow the order of the shapes in the box?
Ring **yes** or **no**.

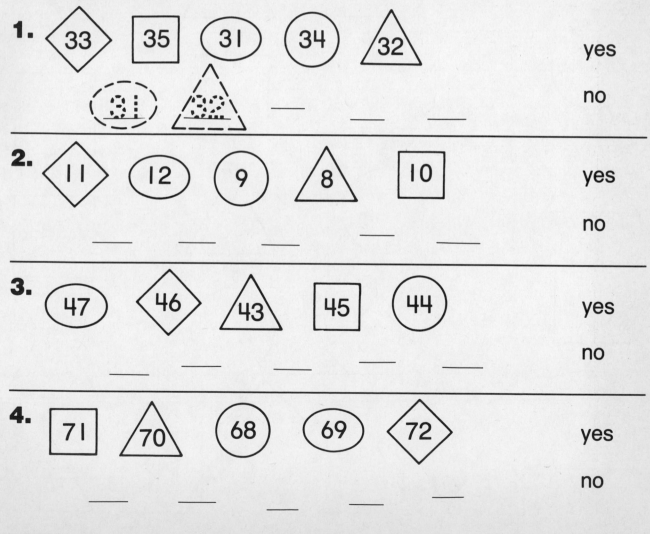

1. 33 35 31 34 32   yes
   31 32 ___ ___ ___   no

2. 11 12 9 8 10   yes
   ___ ___ ___ ___ ___   no

3. 47 46 43 45 44   yes
   ___ ___ ___ ___ ___   no

4. 71 70 68 69 72   yes
   ___ ___ ___ ___ ___   no

Name _____

Number Path

Finish the path. Use the code.

Write the numbers in the shapes.

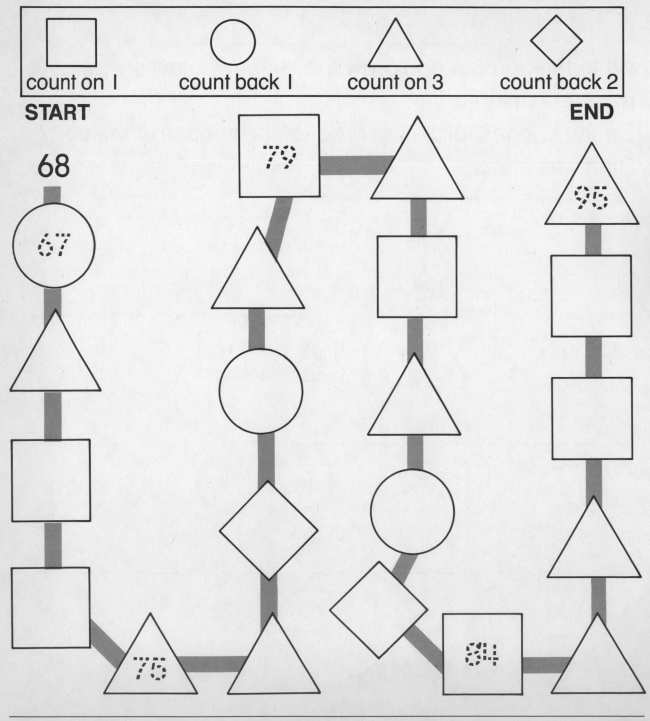

Name _____

Counting in the Land of Unk

These are numbers in order from the land of Unk.

Fill in the blanks.

1. The number after ◇ is _____ .

2. The number before ◇ is _____ .

3. The number between # and ! is _____ .

4. The number after ! is _____ .

5. The number between ◯ and # is _____ .

6. The number before ◯ is _____ .

Name _____

Sizing Up

Write the least and greatest 2-digit numbers
you can make.

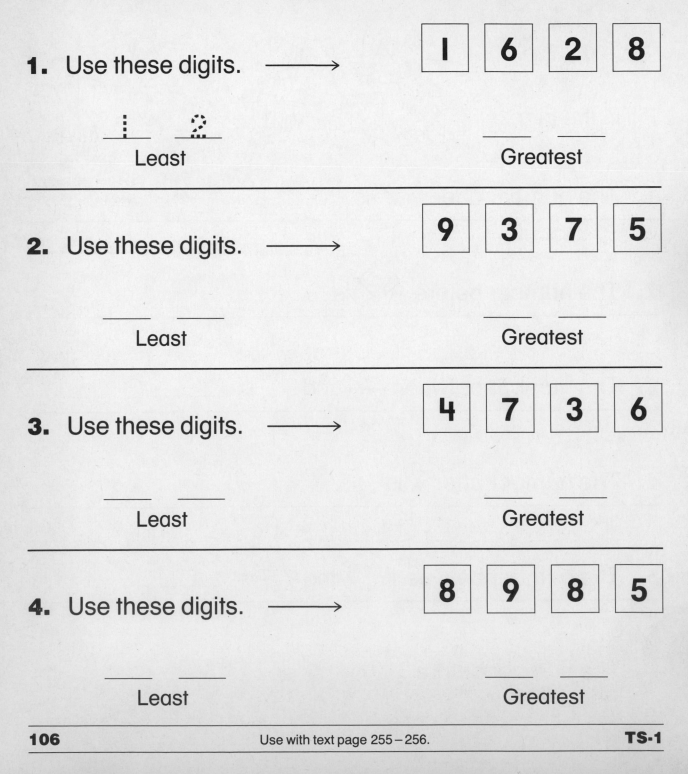

1. Use these digits. ⟶ | 1 | 6 | 2 | 8 |

___ ___   ___ ___
  Least   Greatest

2. Use these digits. ⟶ | 9 | 3 | 7 | 5 |

___ ___   ___ ___
  Least   Greatest

3. Use these digits. ⟶ | 4 | 7 | 3 | 6 |

___ ___   ___ ___
  Least   Greatest

4. Use these digits. ⟶ | 8 | 9 | 8 | 5 |

___ ___   ___ ___
  Least   Greatest

Name _____

Guess and Press

Read each problem.
Write your guess. Then count with your 🖩 .
Write the answer.

1. Press | 1 | 7 | + | 1 | = | = | = | . . .
Stop when you reach 25.

How many times will you press | = | ? _____ guess

How many times did you press | = | ? _____ answer

2. Press | 2 | 0 | + | 1 | 0 | = | = | = | . . .
Stop when you reach 100.

How many times will you press | = | ? _____ guess

How many times did you press | = | ? _____ answer

3. Press | 2 | 5 | + | 1 | 0 | = | = | = | . . .
Stop when you reach 75.

How many times will you press | = | ? _____ guess

How many times did you press | = | ? _____ answer

4. Press | 5 | 0 | + | 5 | = | = | = | . . .
Stop when you reach 100.

How many times will you press | = | ? _____ guess

How many times did you press | = | ? _____ answer

Name _____

Wrong Number

Draw an X on the number that does not belong.
Write the numbers to show the pattern.

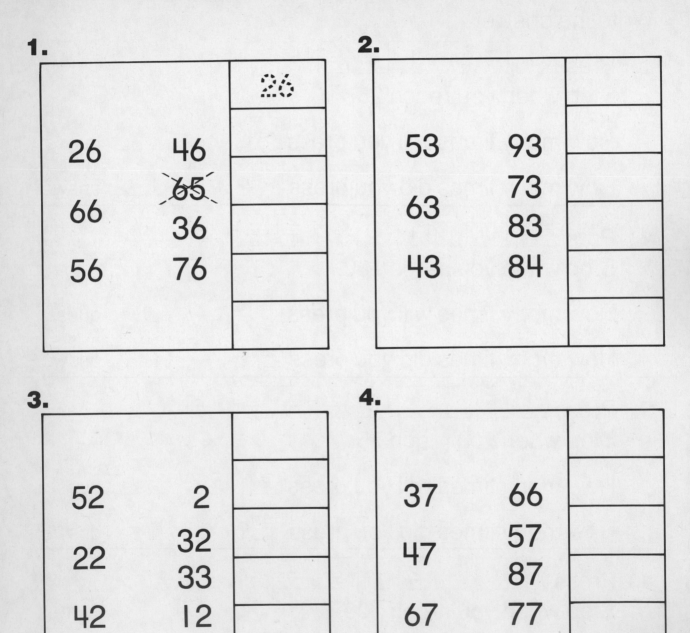

1.

26   46
    ~~65~~
66   36
56   76

26

2.

53   93
      73
63   83
43   84

3.

52   2
      32
22   33
42   12

4.

37   66
      57
47   87
67   77

Name _____

More Patterns

Use your 🖩 to count.

Continue the counting pattern.
Tell the number to count by.

1. Press

| ON/C | 6 | + | = | = | = | = | = | = | = |

6,   12,   18,   24, ____, ____, ____

Count by ____.

2. Press

| ON/C | 9 | + | = | = | = | = | = | = | = |

9,   18,   27,   36, ____, ____, ____

Count by ____.

3. Press

| ON/C | 7 | + | = | = | = | = | = | = | = |

7,   14,   21,   28, ____, ____, ____

Count by ____.

Name _____

Reading Math

> Dear Family,
>   Our class has been studying ordinal numbers. Help your child read the directions. Observe as he or she finds the correct clown.

1. Color the fifth clown's suit [blue] .

2. Draw [red] dots on the second clown's suit.

3. Color the ninth clown's suit [green] .

4. Draw [yellow] stripes on the first clown's suit.

5. Draw a [purple] hat on the tenth clown.

6. Color the third clown's suit [orange] .

Name _____

Pencils and Crayons for Sale

Finish the tables.

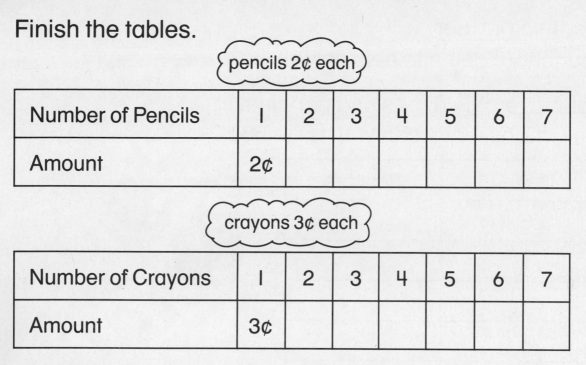

pencils 2¢ each

Number of Pencils	1	2	3	4	5	6	7
Amount	2¢						

crayons 3¢ each

Number of Crayons	1	2	3	4	5	6	7
Amount	3¢						

Use the tables to answer the questions.

1. How much do 4 pencils cost? _____

2. How much do 6 crayons cost? _____

3. If you had 12¢, how many pencils could you buy? _____

4. If you had 15¢, how many crayons could you buy? _____

5. Which costs more, 5 pencils or 4 crayons? Ring one.

　　　　5 pencils　　　　4 crayons

6. If you had 10¢ and wanted to buy the same number of pencils and crayons, how many of each could you buy?

_____ of each

Name _____

Find the Ways

Work with a partner.
Use punchout coins to help solve.

1. You have only dimes and pennies.
How many ways can you make 53¢?

Dimes	Pennies

2. You have 3 dimes and 5 pennies.
Which amounts can you show with your coins? Ring them.

13¢   16¢   34¢   25¢

9¢   30¢   28¢   14¢

15¢   22¢   51¢   37¢

Name _____

How Much More?

Use punchout coins to find how much more is needed.
Draw coins to show.
Write how much money you drew.

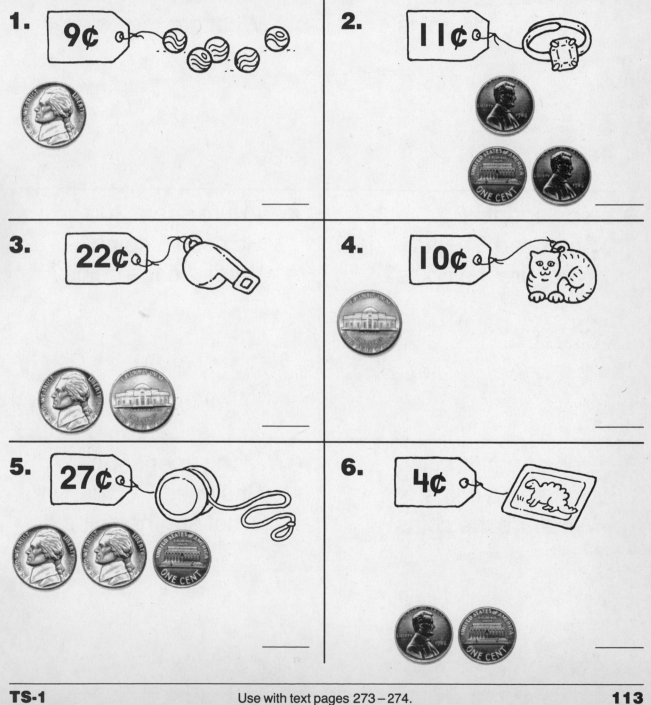

1. 9¢ _____

2. 11¢ _____

3. 22¢ _____

4. 10¢ _____

5. 27¢ _____

6. 4¢ _____

Name _____

Coin Riddles

Draw coins to answer the question.

1. Tom spent 20¢.
He used 4 coins.
What are the coins?

2. Lisa spent 30¢.
She used 4 coins.
What are the coins?

3. Nan spent 40¢.
She used 5 coins.
What are the coins?

4. Arturo spent 30¢.
He used 5 coins.
What are the coins?

5. Ben spent 50¢.
He used 6 coins.
What are the coins?

6. Maria spent 65¢.
She used 7 coins.
What are the coins?

Name _____

How Could You Pay?

What is the least number of coins you could use? Write the numbers.			
1. 39¢	3	1	4
2. 17¢			
3. 28¢			
4. 42¢			
5. 25¢			

Name _____

Spending Money

Use punchout coins to show what you have.
Trade coins to spend.
Draw coins to show what you have left.

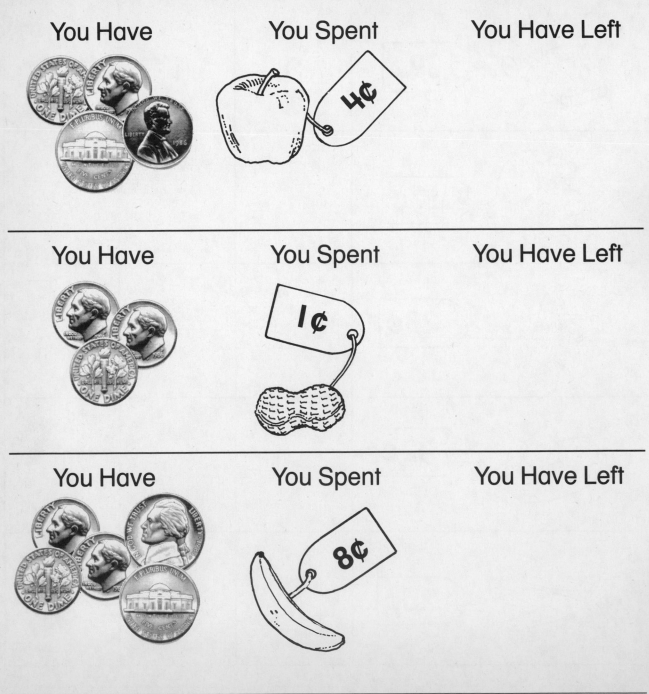

You Have   You Spent   You Have Left

You Have   You Spent   You Have Left

You Have   You Spent   You Have Left

Name _____

Guess My Throw

Look at the total score.

Find out where the third bean bag landed.

Use a ▦ to help you.

Draw a bean bag and write the missing number.

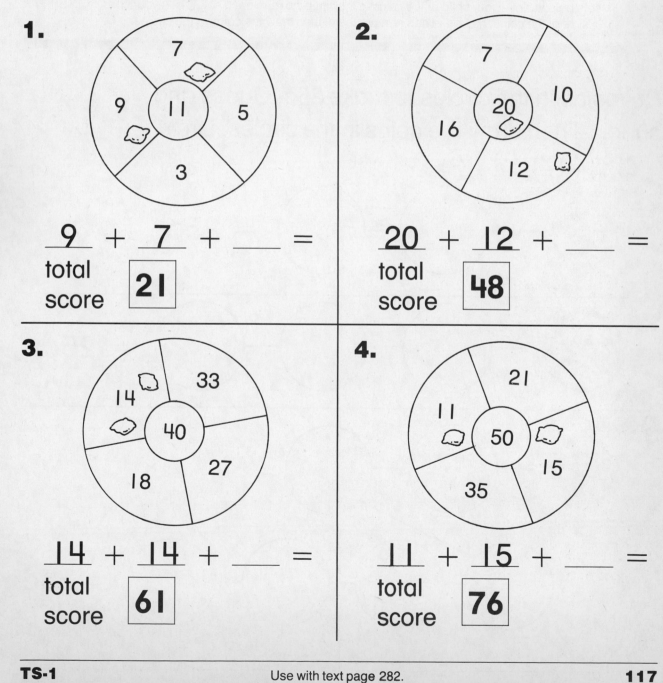

1.

$$\underline{9} + \underline{7} + \underline{} =$$

total score [21]

2.

$$\underline{20} + \underline{12} + \underline{} =$$

total score [48]

3.

$$\underline{14} + \underline{14} + \underline{} =$$

total score [61]

4.

$$\underline{11} + \underline{15} + \underline{} =$$

total score [76]

Name _____

Quarters and Other Coins

Dear Family,
    Our class has just completed a lesson on counting with quarters and other coins. This activity will help your child understand the values of a quarter, dime, nickel, and penny. Please provide 5 pennies, 5 nickels, and 5 dimes. Help your child make various combinations that equal 25¢. Then observe as he or she finds the missing coins in the sets below. Have your child place coins in the circles to form each set. When your child is sure of the coins, he or she can remove them, then draw the coins in the circles.

Put coins in the circles to make 25¢. Guess and check. Then draw the coins in the circles. Draw ⓢ5¢ , ⓘ1¢ , or ⓣ10¢ .

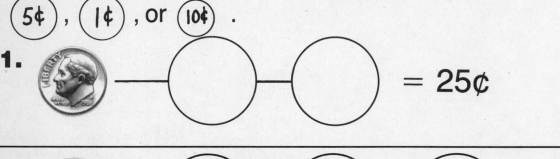

1. ◯ — ◯ — ◯ = 25¢

2. ◯ — ◯ — ◯ = 25¢

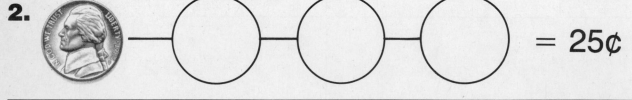

3. ◯ — ◯
    ◯ — ◯ — ◯ — ◯ = 25¢

Use with text pages 283–284.   TS-1

Name _____

Pick a Purse

Guess which purse has more money. Ring it.
Count to check. Write the amounts.

1.

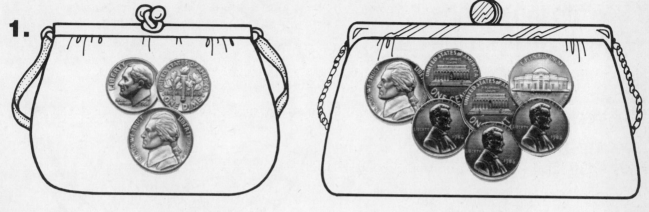

_____ ¢   _____ ¢

2.

_____ ¢   _____ ¢

3.

_____ ¢   _____ ¢

Name _____

It's About Time

Look at the clock.

1. Write the number missing from the ☐.

2. Write the number missing from the △.

3. Write the numbers missing from the ○.

4. Write **minute** and **hour** under the hand that shows it.

short hand shows   long hand shows

_____   _____

5. Which hand goes around faster?
    Is it the **minute** hand or the **hour** hand?

the _____ hand

Name _____

Time Goes By

Read the problem. Use your punchout
clock to find the answer. Draw
hands on the clock to show the answer.

1. Mark finishes dinner at 6 o'clock.
He reads his books for 3 hours.
Then he goes to bed.
When does Mark go to bed?

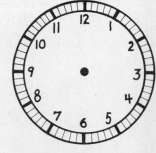

2. Kay went to Jamal's house.
She has to be home in 2 hours.
She left home at 1 o'clock.
When does Kay have to be home?

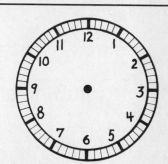

3. It is 2 o'clock. Tim's birthday
party starts in 4 hours.
When does the party start?

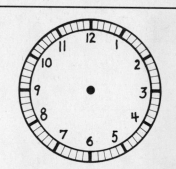

4. Anita has dinner 4 hours after
she gets home from school. She
gets home from school at 3 o'clock.
When does Anita have dinner?

Name _____

Time Sense

Match each action with the one that takes
about the same amount of time.
Draw lines to match.

1. tying your shoes

making a quilt

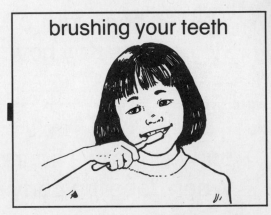

2. growing an inch

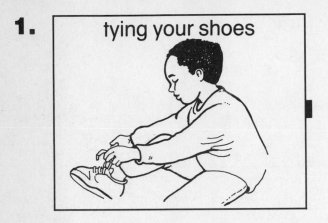

brushing your teeth

3. eating dinner

doing your homework

Name _____

Time on My Hands

About what time does it happen?
Draw the hands on the clock.

1. Wake up

2. Eat breakfast

3. Go to school

4. Eat lunch

5. Eat supper

6. Go to bed

Name _____

Time and Time Again

Read the problem. Use your punchout clock
to find the answer. Write the time.

1. Amy leaves home at 7:30. She gets
to school one half hour later.
When does Amy get to school?

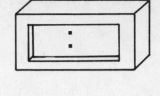

2. Ari started to eat lunch at 12:00.
He finished eating one half hour later.
When did Ari finish eating lunch?

3. Nora arrived at Pat's house at 3:30.
She left one hour later.
When did Nora leave Pat's house?

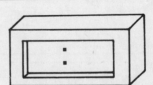

4. Cal was told to be home by 5:30.
He arrived home one hour early.
When did Cal arrive home?

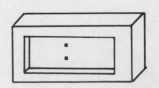

Name _____

Choose the Date

Mrs. Chin's first-grade class is planning a trip to the zoo. Help the students find a date for the trip. Put an X on dates the class cannot go. Circle the date they can go.

April						
Sunday	Monday	Tuesday	Wednesday	Thursday	Friday	Saturday
		1	2	3	4	5
6	7	8	9	10	11	12
13	14	15	16	17	18	19
20	21	22	23	24	25	26
27	28	29	30			

1. The class will go on a school day.

2. The zoo is closed Mondays and Wednesdays.

3. The school bus is not available on Tuesdays and Thursdays.

4. The fourth day of the month is a holiday.

5. The third Friday is a holiday.

6. The class play is planned for April 11. _____

Name the month and date for the class trip. _____

Name _____

Wagon Ride

There are 3 children. There is 1 wagon.

Two children can play at a time.

One child can ride and one child can pull.

Find 6 different ways the children can ride and pull.

List the ways.

Wagon Ride

	Child Pulling	Child Riding
1.	Leo	
2.		
3.		
4.		
5.		
6.		

Name _____

Who Am I?

Use and counters. Write the answer.

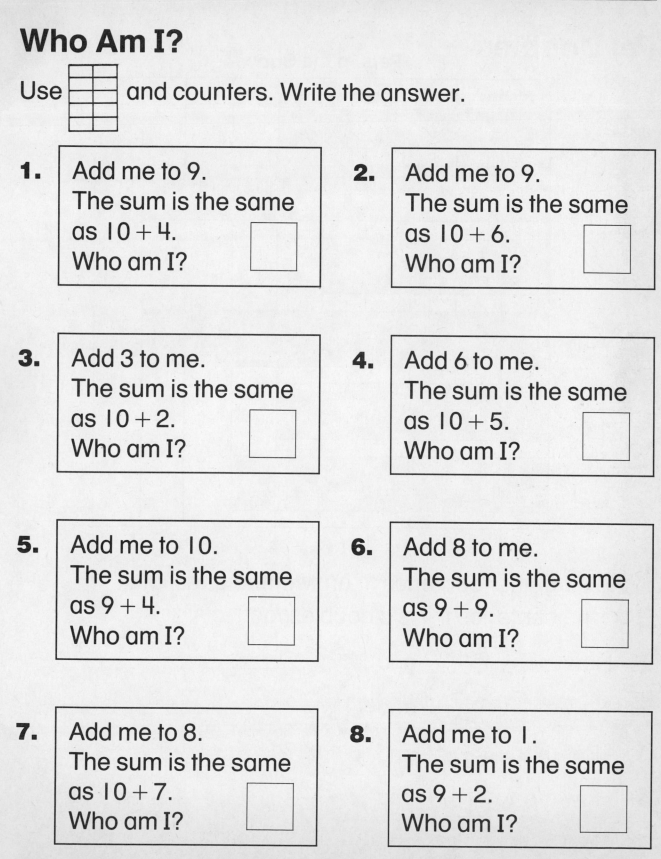

1. Add me to 9.
The sum is the same
as 10 + 4.
Who am I? ▢

2. Add me to 9.
The sum is the same
as 10 + 6.
Who am I? ▢

3. Add 3 to me.
The sum is the same
as 10 + 2.
Who am I? ▢

4. Add 6 to me.
The sum is the same
as 10 + 5.
Who am I? ▢

5. Add me to 10.
The sum is the same
as 9 + 4.
Who am I? ▢

6. Add 8 to me.
The sum is the same
as 9 + 9.
Who am I? ▢

7. Add me to 8.
The sum is the same
as 10 + 7.
Who am I? ▢

8. Add me to 1.
The sum is the same
as 9 + 2.
Who am I? ▢

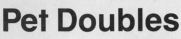

Name _____

Pet Doubles

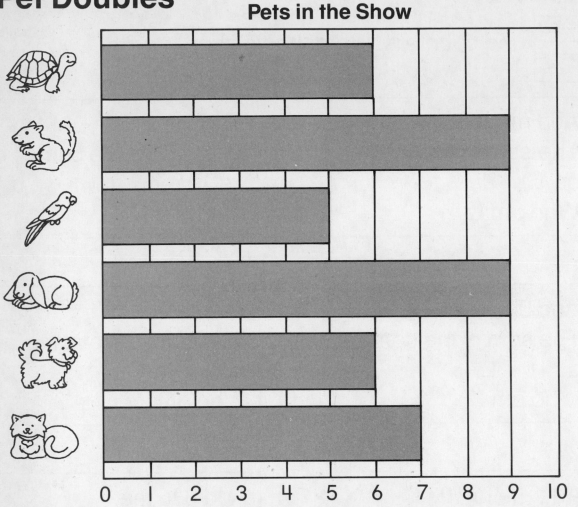

Pets in the Show

Write a number sentence to answer the question.

Ring the sentence if it is a doubles fact.

1. How many 🐢 and 🦜 ? _____

2. How many 🐿 and 🐶 ? _____

3. How many 🐢 and 🐩 ? _____

4. How many 🐱 and 🦜 ? _____

5. How many 🐶 and 🐱 ? _____

Name _____

What to Buy?

Solve. Ring the answer.

1. Jane spent 11¢.
Which toys did she buy?

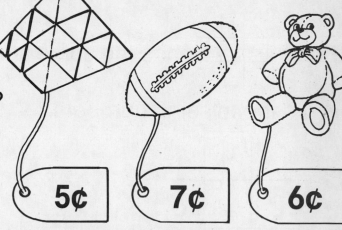

5¢   7¢   6¢

2. Ron bought 15 apples.
Which bags did he buy?

5 apples   9 apples   6 apples

3. Sara had 13¢.
Now she has 8¢.
What did she buy?

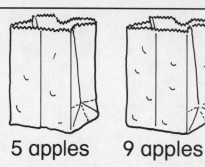

5¢   4¢   3¢

4. Tom put 12 shells
into two piles.
Which ones are
Tom's piles?

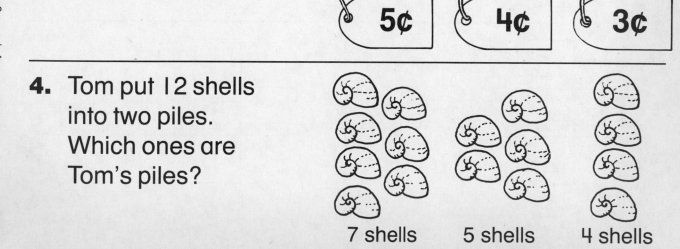

7 shells   5 shells   4 shells

Name _____

Missing Numbers

Each ⊞ has the same sum across and down.

Write the missing numbers.

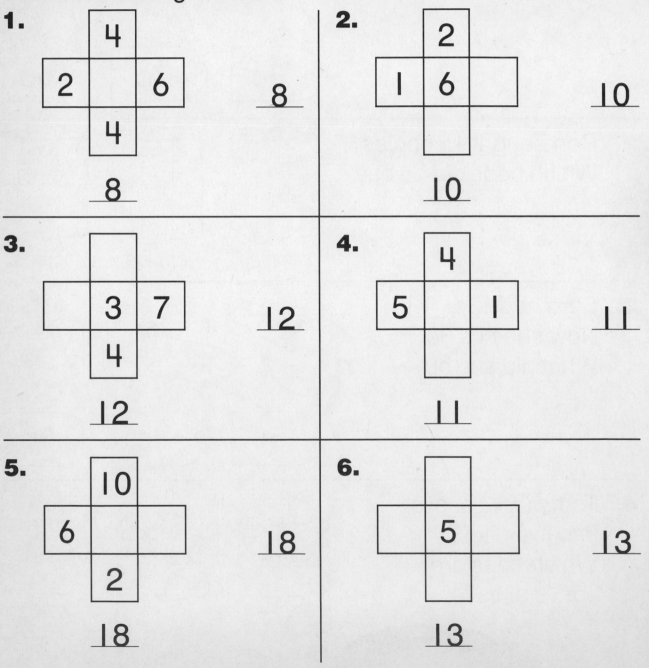

1.

4
2 · 6   8
4

8

2.

2
1 · 6   10
·

10

3.

·
3 · 7   12
4

12

4.

4
5 · 1   11
·

11

5.

10
6 · ·   18
2

18

6.

·
· 5 ·   13
·

13

Name _____

Money Riddles

Solve each riddle.
Write a money amount on each coin.

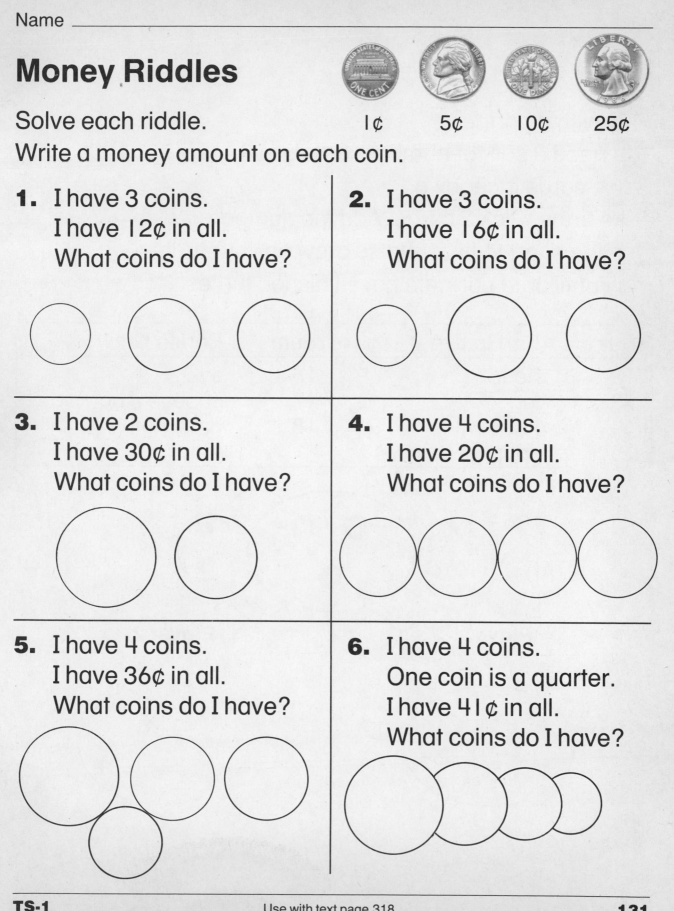

1¢   5¢   10¢   25¢

1. I have 3 coins.
I have 12¢ in all.
What coins do I have?

○ ○ ○

2. I have 3 coins.
I have 16¢ in all.
What coins do I have?

○ ○ ○

3. I have 2 coins.
I have 30¢ in all.
What coins do I have?

○ ○

4. I have 4 coins.
I have 20¢ in all.
What coins do I have?

○ ○ ○ ○

5. I have 4 coins.
I have 36¢ in all.
What coins do I have?

○ ○ ○
  ○

6. I have 4 coins.
One coin is a quarter.
I have 41¢ in all.
What coins do I have?

○ ○ ○ ○

Name _____

Draw a Turtle

Play with a partner.

You need 2 sets of number cards 6 to 9.

Place cards facedown.

Take turns. Pick 2 cards. Add the numbers.

Use the chart to find what to draw on your turtle.

Play until both partners have finished turtles.

Sum	Part to Draw	Sum	Part to Draw
12	head	16	eye
13	leg	17	choose a part
14	tail	18	draw nothing
15	spot		

Player 1   **Player 2**

Name _____

Tic-Tac-Toe

Play with a partner.
Choose X or O. Take turns.
Pick an addition fact and write the
answer. Find the answer on the board.
Draw an X or O.
Three X's or three O's in a row wins.

18	11	16
17	14	12
10	15	13

$$\begin{array}{r} 5 \\ +9 \\ \hline \end{array} \qquad \begin{array}{r} 7 \\ +6 \\ \hline \end{array} \qquad \begin{array}{r} 9 \\ +8 \\ \hline \end{array} \qquad \begin{array}{r} 9 \\ +9 \\ \hline \end{array} \qquad \begin{array}{r} 3 \\ +7 \\ \hline \end{array}$$

$$\begin{array}{r} 4 \\ +8 \\ \hline \end{array} \qquad \begin{array}{r} 7 \\ +7 \\ \hline \end{array} \qquad \begin{array}{r} 1 \\ +9 \\ \hline \end{array} \qquad \begin{array}{r} 8 \\ +8 \\ \hline \end{array} \qquad \begin{array}{r} 6 \\ +8 \\ \hline \end{array}$$

$$\begin{array}{r} 5 \\ +7 \\ \hline \end{array} \qquad \begin{array}{r} 7 \\ +8 \\ \hline \end{array} \qquad \begin{array}{r} 8 \\ +3 \\ \hline \end{array} \qquad \begin{array}{r} 7 \\ +9 \\ \hline \end{array} \qquad \begin{array}{r} 9 \\ +6 \\ \hline \end{array}$$

Name _____

Find the Patterns

Find the sums. Look for patterns. Complete
the next two additions.

1.
$$\begin{array}{r} 6 \\ +4 \\ \hline \end{array}$$
$$\begin{array}{r} 6 \\ +5 \\ \hline \end{array}$$
$$\begin{array}{r} 6 \\ +6 \\ \hline \end{array}$$
$$\begin{array}{r} 6 \\ +\boxed{} \\ \hline \end{array}$$
$$\begin{array}{r} 6 \\ +\boxed{} \\ \hline \end{array}$$

2.
$$\begin{array}{r} 3 \\ +5 \\ \hline \end{array}$$
$$\begin{array}{r} 4 \\ +5 \\ \hline \end{array}$$
$$\begin{array}{r} 5 \\ +5 \\ \hline \end{array}$$
$$\begin{array}{r} 6 \\ +\boxed{} \\ \hline \end{array}$$
$$\begin{array}{r} \boxed{} \\ +5 \\ \hline \end{array}$$

3.
$$\begin{array}{r} 9 \\ +7 \\ \hline \end{array}$$
$$\begin{array}{r} 8 \\ +7 \\ \hline \end{array}$$
$$\begin{array}{r} 7 \\ +7 \\ \hline \end{array}$$
$$\begin{array}{r} 6 \\ +\boxed{} \\ \hline \end{array}$$
$$\begin{array}{r} \boxed{} \\ +\boxed{} \\ \hline \end{array}$$

4.
$$\begin{array}{r} 3 \\ +2 \\ \hline \end{array}$$
$$\begin{array}{r} 4 \\ +3 \\ \hline \end{array}$$
$$\begin{array}{r} 5 \\ +4 \\ \hline \end{array}$$
$$\begin{array}{r} 6 \\ +\boxed{} \\ \hline \end{array}$$
$$\begin{array}{r} \boxed{} \\ +\boxed{} \\ \hline \end{array}$$

Name _____

Age Sense

Read each clue.
Ring the number on the chart that makes sense.

1. Ann will be 7 years old next year.

2. Brian is double Ann's age.

3. Carlos is 5 years younger than Brian.

4. Debra is 4 years older than Carlos.

5. Eric is 3 years younger than Debra.

Ages		
Ann	6	8
Brian	4	12
Carlos	15	7
Debra	11	3
Eric	14	8

Use the chart above to answer the questions.

6. How much older is Eric than Ann? _____ years

7. How much younger is Ann than Debra? _____ years

8. Fran is the age of Ann and Carlos combined. How old is Fran? _____ years

9. Gary will be Brian's age in 2 years. How old is Gary? _____ years

Name _____

A Neat Trick

Add or subtract.
Look for doubles.

Think 6 + 6.

1. 6 $+ 2 + 4 =$ ___

2. 14 $- 3 - 4 =$ ___

3. 9 $+ 5 + 4 =$ ___

4. 18 $- 6 - 3 =$ ___

5. $6 +$ 8 $+ 2 =$ ___

6. 14 $- 2 - 5 =$ ___

7. $3 + 4 +$ 7 $=$ ___

Think 12 − 6.

12 $- 1 - 5 =$ ___

5 $+ 2 + 3 =$ ___

16 $- 4 - 4 =$ ___

$1 +$ 7 $+ 6 =$ ___

12 $- 3 - 3 =$ ___

18 $- 2 - 7 =$ ___

16 $- 2 - 6 =$ ___

Name _____

Mystery Number

Read each clue.
Each clue will help you cross out
a number.
The number that is left is the mystery number.

1. It is **not** 14 − 9.

2. It is **not** 17 − 9.

3. It is **not** 10 − 9.

4. It is **not** 16 − 9.

5. It is **not** 13 − 9.

6. It is **not** 18 − 9.

7. It is **not** 11 − 9.

8. It is **not** 12 − 9.

The mystery number is _____.

Name _____

The Pet Show

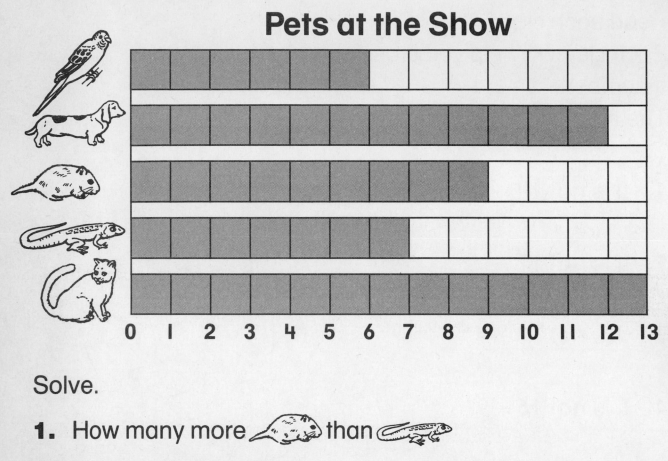

Pets at the Show

Solve.

1. How many more 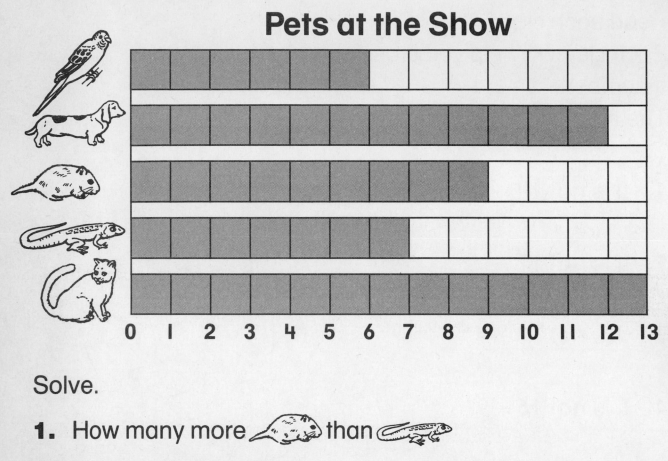 than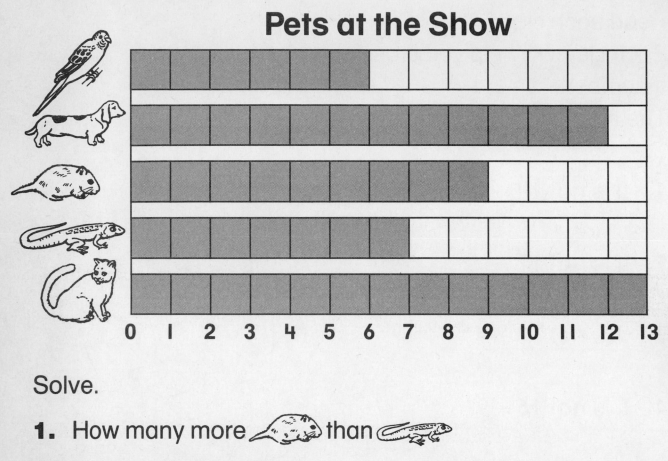

were at the show? _____

2. How many more 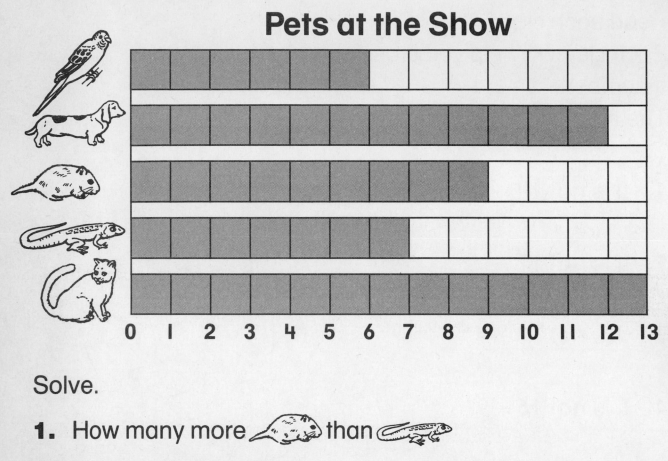 than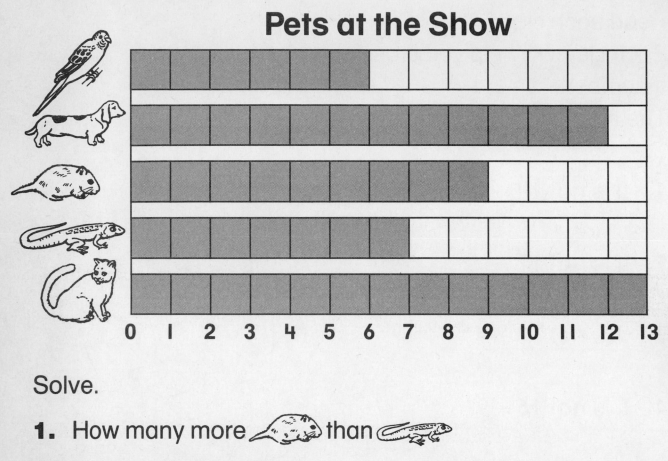

were at the show? _____

3. How many more than

 were at the show? _____

4. How many more than

were at the show? _____

Name _____

Use a Calculator

Find the doubles.

Use your 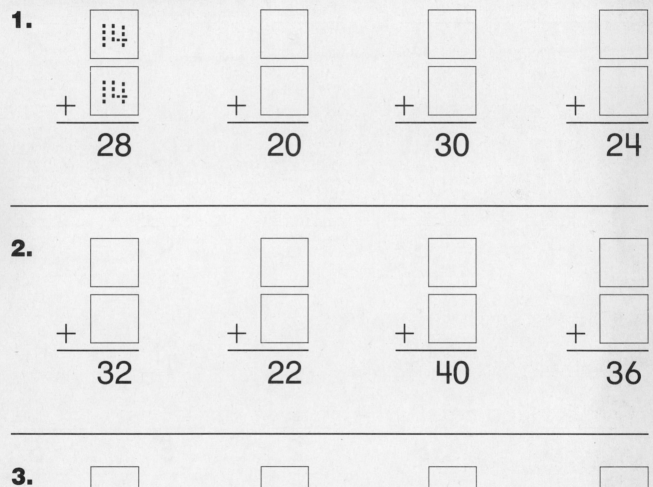 to guess and check.
Write the numbers.

1.

14
14

+

28

+

20

+

30

+

24

2.

+

32

+

22

+

40

+

36

3.

+

44

+

26

+

42

+

50

Name _____

What Number?

What number was subtracted, 4, 5, or 6?

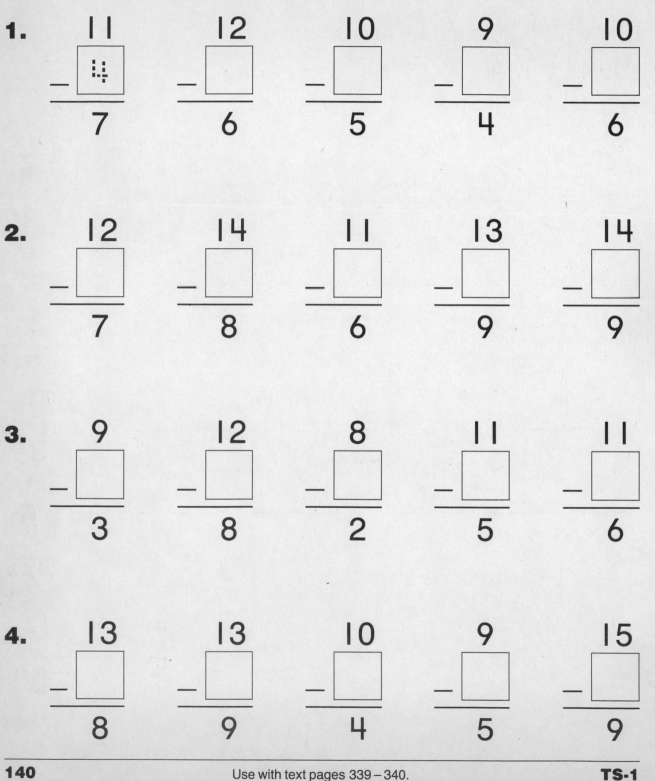

1.

11	12	10	9	10
− ▦	− ☐	☐ −	☐ −	☐ −
7	6	5	4	6

2.

12	14	11	13	14
− ☐	− ☐	− ☐	− ☐	− ☐
7	8	6	9	9

3.

9	12	8	11	11
− ☐	− ☐	− ☐	− ☐	− ☐
3	8	2	5	6

4.

13	13	10	9	15
− ☐	− ☐	− ☐	− ☐	− ☐
8	9	4	5	9

Name _____

Patterns

Work with a partner. Use a ▦ .
Write the answers.
Tell your partner the pattern you see.

1.
$$13 - 9$$ $$13 - 8$$ $$13 - 7$$ $$13 - 6$$ $$13 - 5$$

2.
$$16 - 9$$ $$16 - 8$$ $$16 - 7$$ $$16 - 6$$ $$16 - 5$$

3.
$$14 - 9$$ $$14 - 8$$ $$14 - 7$$ $$14 - 6$$ $$14 - 5$$

4.
$$15 - 9$$ $$15 - 8$$ $$15 - 7$$ $$15 - 6$$ $$15 - 5$$

5.
$$17 - 9$$ $$17 - 8$$ $$17 - 7$$ $$17 - 6$$ $$17 - 5$$

Name _____

Pair of Facts

Work with a partner.
Guess which fact in each pair has
the smaller difference.
Tell your partner how you made that guess.
Color that kite.
Subtract both facts to check.

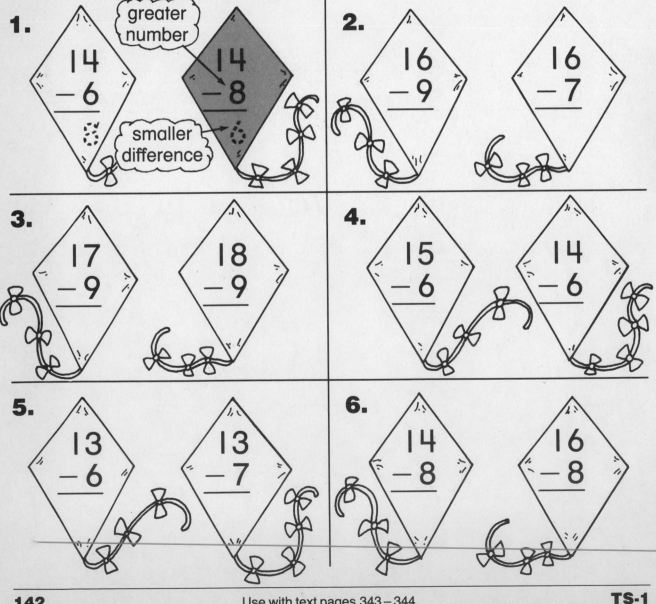

1.

greater number

14
− 6

14
− 8

smaller difference

2.

16
− 9

16
− 7

3.

17
− 9

18
− 9

4.

15
− 6

14
− 6

5.

13
− 6

13
− 7

6.

14
− 8

16
− 8

Name _____

Find the Facts

> Dear Family,
>   Our class is studying addition and subtraction facts to 18. You can help your child review these facts by playing the game below. Allow him or her to use small objects, such as buttons, if needed.

Find the hidden facts. Go across or down. Take turns. Ring the facts. There are 22 facts. The first one is done for you.

16	7	9	12	13	18	2
8	2	2	7	9	9	0
8	4	11	4	5	9	2
6	6	12	4	14	12	3
10	2	8	7	6	7	13
2	4	13	11	8	4	5
2	6	8	6	9	15	6
9	4	5	10	2	8	11

Name _____

Across the Meadow

Find the ways Randy Rabbit can get home.
Write the ways.

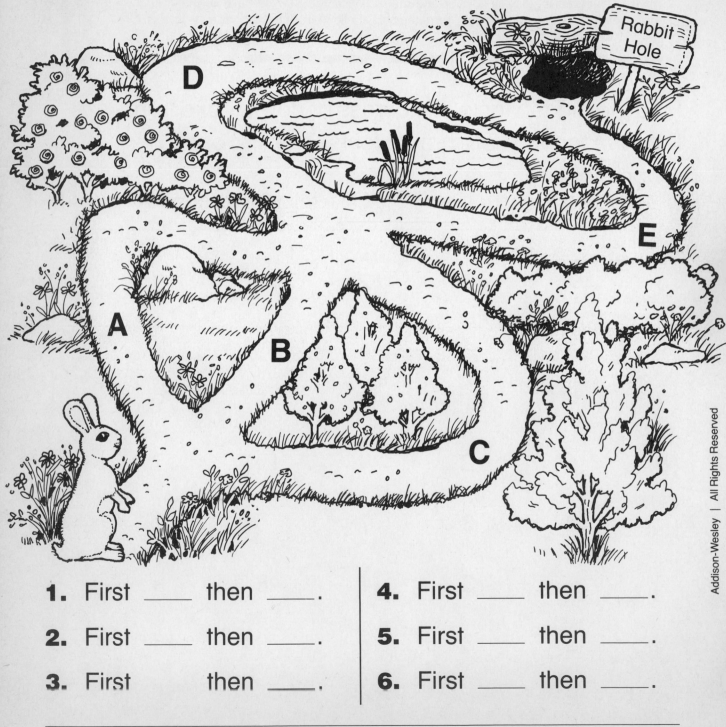

1. First ____ then ____ .

2. First ____ then ____ .

3. First ____ then ____ .

4. First ____ then ____ .

5. First ____ then ____ .

6. First ____ then ____ .

Name _____

Missing Addends

What number was added?
Count on 1, 2, or 3.
Write the missing number.

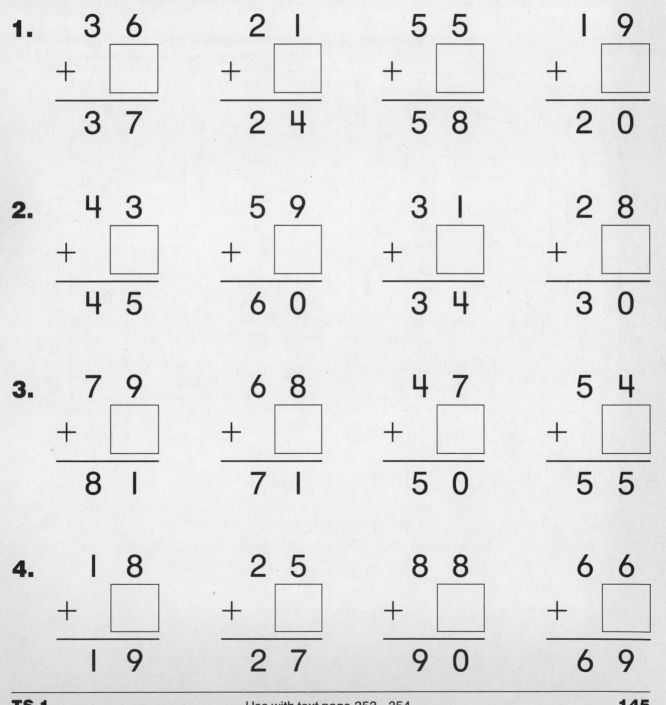

1. 3 6   2 1   5 5   1 9
   + ☐   + ☐   + ☐   + ☐
   3 7   2 4   5 8   2 0

2. 4 3   5 9   3 1   2 8
   + ☐   + ☐   + ☐   + ☐
   4 5   6 0   3 4   3 0

3. 7 9   6 8   4 7   5 4
   + ☐   + ☐   + ☐   + ☐
   8 1   7 1   5 0   5 5

4. 1 8   2 5   8 8   6 6
   + ☐   + ☐   + ☐   + ☐
   1 9   2 7   9 0   6 9

Name _____

Groups of Ten

Dear Family,
  Our class is learning how to add 1-digit numbers to 2-digit numbers. We are using the strategy of first making a ten. For example, to add 6 to 26, first add 4 to make 30, and then add the extra 2. (32) You can help your child develop skill in using this strategy. Use small objects to set up these groups: 17, 24, 19, and 22. Have your child add objects to each group to make the next ten, write how many were added, and color the picture according to the directions.

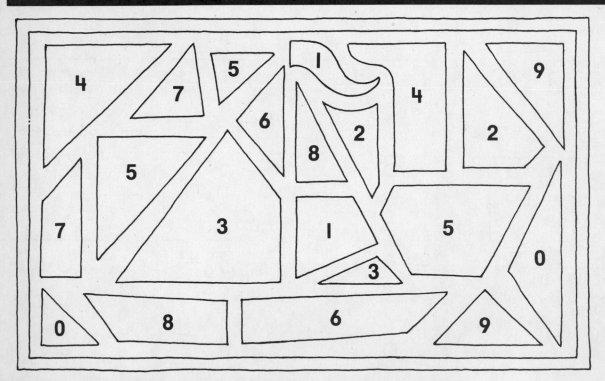

Make a ten. Write the number.

Start with 17. Add _____ to make a ten.

Start with 24. Add _____ to make a ten.

Start with 19. Add _____ to make a ten.

Start with 22. Add _____ to make a ten.

Color the shapes that have the numbers you added.

Name _____

Use Your Head

Use mental math to solve.
Ring your answers.

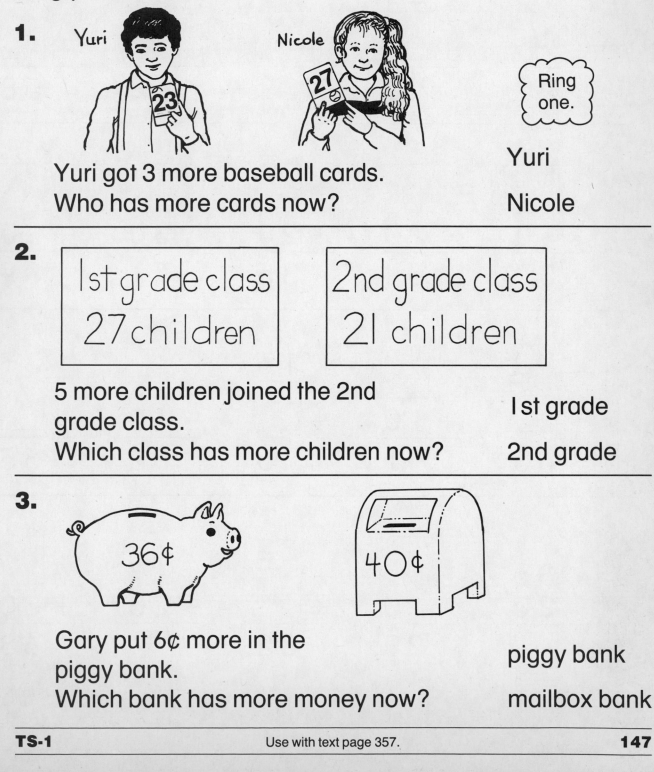

1. Yuri　Nicole

Yuri got 3 more baseball cards.
Who has more cards now?

Ring
one.

Yuri

Nicole

2.

| 1st grade class | 2nd grade class |
| 27 children | 21 children |

5 more children joined the 2nd
grade class.
Which class has more children now?

1st grade

2nd grade

3.

36¢　40¢

Gary put 6¢ more in the
piggy bank.
Which bank has more money now?

piggy bank

mailbox bank

Name _____

What Is Missing?

Write the missing number.

1.

$$\begin{array}{r} 13 \\ + \boxed{10} \\ \hline 23 \end{array} \qquad \begin{array}{r} 26 \\ + \boxed{} \\ \hline 46 \end{array} \qquad \begin{array}{r} 19 \\ + \boxed{} \\ \hline 39 \end{array} \qquad \begin{array}{r} 32 \\ + \boxed{} \\ \hline 62 \end{array} \qquad \begin{array}{r} 48 \\ + \boxed{} \\ \hline 58 \end{array}$$

2.

$$\begin{array}{r} \boxed{} \\ + 10 \\ \hline 37 \end{array} \qquad \begin{array}{r} \boxed{} \\ + 20 \\ \hline 64 \end{array} \qquad \begin{array}{r} \boxed{} \\ + 20 \\ \hline 35 \end{array} \qquad \begin{array}{r} \boxed{} \\ + 30 \\ \hline 71 \end{array} \qquad \begin{array}{r} \boxed{} \\ + 20 \\ \hline 89 \end{array}$$

3.

$$\begin{array}{r} 43 \\ + \boxed{} \\ \hline 63 \end{array} \qquad \begin{array}{r} \boxed{} \\ + 10 \\ \hline 41 \end{array} \qquad \begin{array}{r} 16 \\ + \boxed{} \\ \hline 46 \end{array} \qquad \begin{array}{r} \boxed{} \\ + 10 \\ \hline 82 \end{array} \qquad \begin{array}{r} 35 \\ + \boxed{} \\ \hline 55 \end{array}$$

4.

$$\begin{array}{r} 36 \\ + 20 \\ \hline \boxed{} \end{array} \qquad \begin{array}{r} \boxed{} \\ + 10 \\ \hline 29 \end{array} \qquad \begin{array}{r} 52 \\ + \boxed{} \\ \hline 82 \end{array} \qquad \begin{array}{r} 17 \\ + 20 \\ \hline \boxed{} \end{array} \qquad \begin{array}{r} \boxed{} \\ + 30 \\ \hline 68 \end{array}$$

Name _____

More or Less?

Ring the correct estimate.

1. 42 + 16

less than 50

(more than 50)

2. 13 + 21

less than 40

more than 40

3. 12 + 37

less than 50

more than 50

4. 25 + 22

less than 40

more than 40

5. 36 + 23

less than 50

more than 50

6. 41 + 34

less than 80

more than 80

7. 31 + 35

less than 70

more than 70

8. 43 + 44

less than 80

more than 80

Name _____

How Many Were Taken Out?

Write how many were taken out.

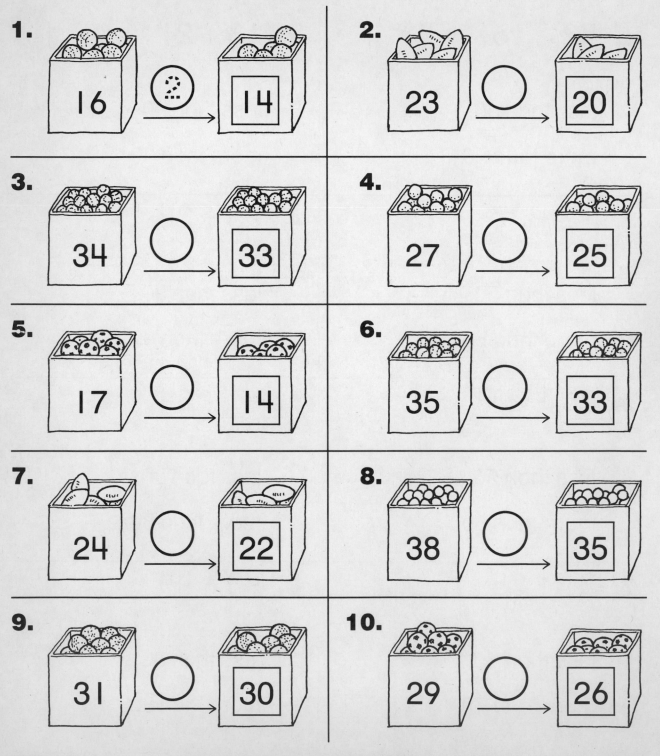

1. 16 → ② → 14

2. 23 → ○ → 20

3. 34 → ○ → 33

4. 27 → ○ → 25

5. 17 → ○ → 14

6. 35 → ○ → 33

7. 24 → ○ → 22

8. 38 → ○ → 35

9. 31 → ○ → 30

10. 29 → ○ → 26

Name _____

What Is Missing?

Write the missing number.

1.

25	37	42	68	54
− [10]	− □	− □	− □	− □
15	17	32	38	34

2.

□	□	□	□	□
− 10	− 20	− 30	− 10	− 20
12	21	15	53	36

3.

38	□	49	□	52
− □	− 30	− □	− 20	− □
18	25	39	47	22

4.

43	51	□	64	46
− 10	− □	− 30	− 20	− □
□	31	15	□	16

Name ___

Crossnumber Puzzle

Dear Family,
   Our class is learning how to subtract tens and ones. Provide your child with 8 dimes to use as tens and 9 pennies to use as ones. Help your child complete this crossnumber puzzle.

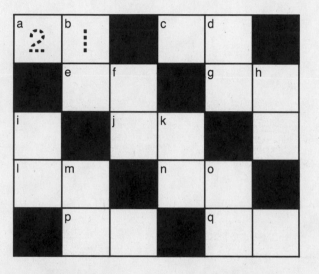

Across

a. $41 - 20$
c. $57 - 10$
e. $83 - 30$
g. $24 - 12$
j. $97 - 21$
l. $74 - 13$
n. $48 - 24$
p. $79 - 25$
q. $68 - 32$

Down

b. $38 - 23$
d. $85 - 14$
f. $57 - 20$
h. $48 - 25$
i. $88 - 42$
k. $74 - 12$
m. $49 - 34$
o. $67 - 24$

Name _____

Cookie Cutouts

Draw a picture to solve. Write the answer.

1. Andy made 5 circle cookies. He made 1 less square cookie than circle cookies. He made 1 less triangle cookie than square cookies.

How many cookies did he make in all? _____ cookies

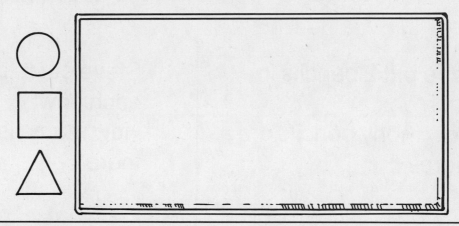

2. Monica made 4 heart cookies. She made 2 more star cookies than heart cookies. She made 2 less tree cookies than star cookies.

How many cookies did she make in all? _____ cookies

Name _____

Two by Two

Use mental math. Write how many in all.

1.

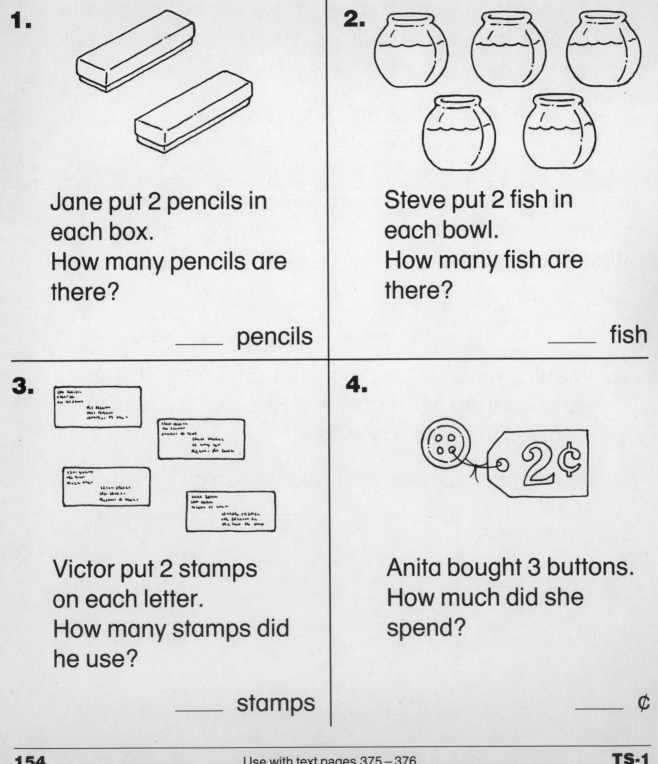

Jane put 2 pencils in
each box.
How many pencils are
there?

_____ pencils

2.

Steve put 2 fish in
each bowl.
How many fish are
there?

_____ fish

3.

Victor put 2 stamps
on each letter.
How many stamps did
he use?

_____ stamps

4.

Anita bought 3 buttons.
How much did she
spend?

_____ ¢

Name _____

Stamp Sets

Write how much each set costs.

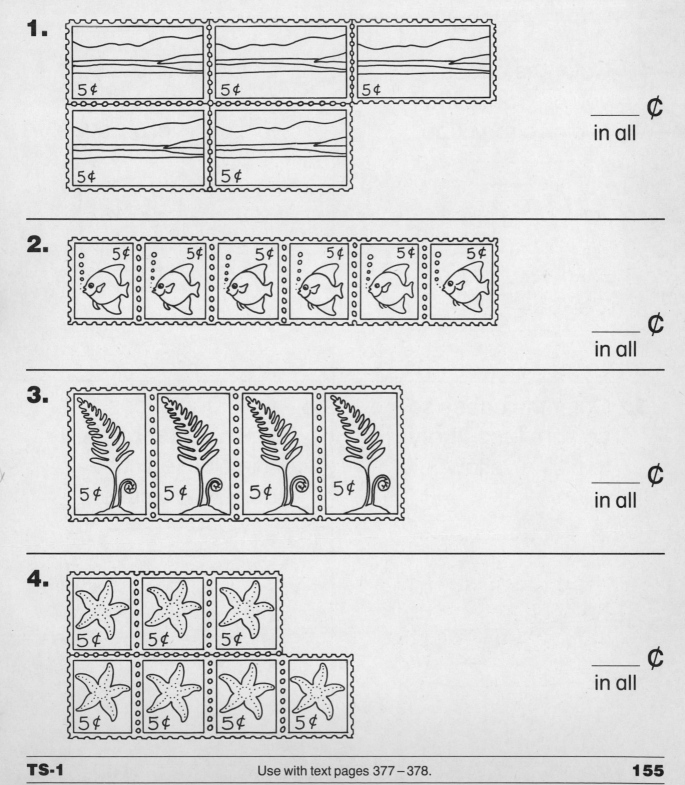

1.

5¢ 5¢ 5¢

5¢ 5¢

_____ ¢
in all

2.

5¢ 5¢ 5¢ 5¢ 5¢ 5¢

_____ ¢
in all

3.

5¢ 5¢ 5¢ 5¢

_____ ¢
in all

4.

5¢ 5¢ 5¢

5¢ 5¢ 5¢ 5¢

_____ ¢
in all

Name. _____

In the Bag

Follow the directions.
Color the cubes. Use red and yellow.

1. Color the cubes so you are **more likely** to pick a red cube.

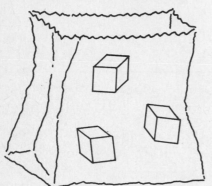

2. Color the cubes so you are **more likely** to pick a yellow cube.

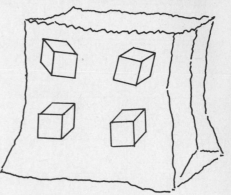

3. Color the cubes so you are **less likely** to pick a yellow cube.

4. Color the cubes so you are **just as likely** to pick a red cube as a yellow cube.

Name _____

Sharing to Make Equal Groups

Which 🖍 can be shared equally by 👤👤👤 ?
Which 🖍 can be shared equally by 👤👤👤👤 ?
Use counters to help you.
Draw lines to match.

Name _____

Sports Store

Make equal groups.

Color the graph to show how many boxes.

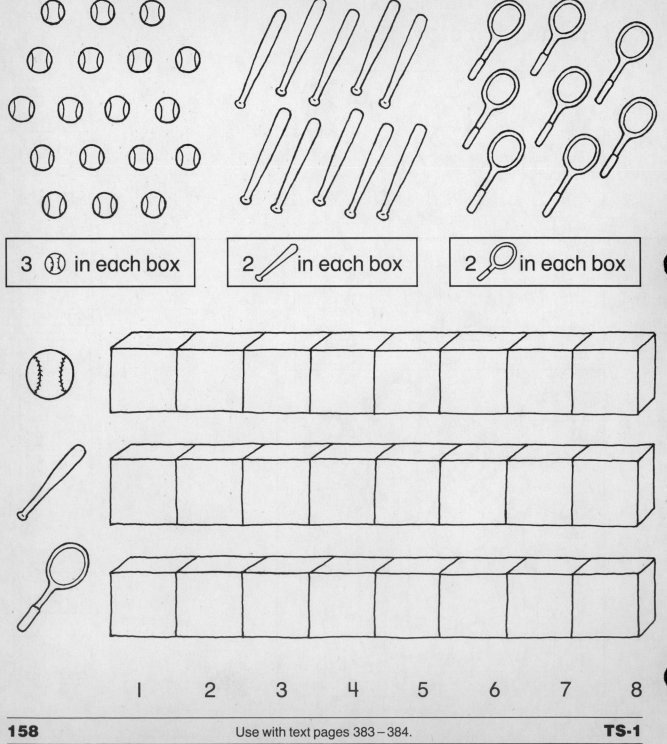

3 🎾 in each box   2 🏏 in each box   2 🎾 in each box

| | 1 | 2 | 3 | 4 | 5 | 6 | 7 | 8 |

Name _____

Different Halves

Work with a partner.
Draw and color the shape that comes next.
Talk about what you do.

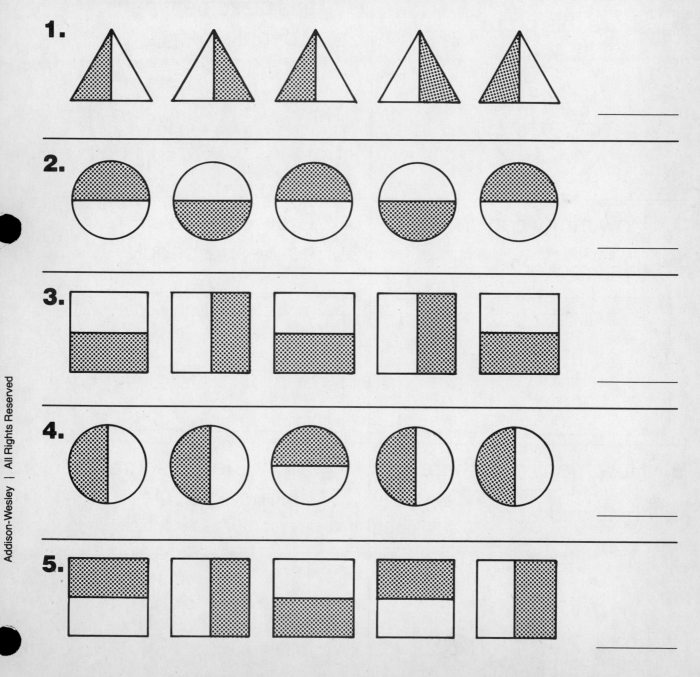

1.

2.

3.

4.

5.

Name _____

Sharing

Write the number or draw lines.

1. How many friends can

share this pizza? ____

2. Draw a line to share this pizza between 2 people.

3. How many can share

this cracker? ____

4. Draw a line to share between 2 people.

5. How many can share

this sandwich? ____

6. Draw lines to share among 4 people.

Name _____

Draw and Color

Draw the fruit each child has.
Color to show the fraction.

1. Allie has 4 .

$\frac{3}{4}$ of them are green.

How many are green?

_____

2. Tony has 8 .

$\frac{1}{4}$ of them are red.

How many are red?

_____

3. Lou has 3 .

$\frac{2}{3}$ of them are green.

How many are green?

_____

4. Sam has 6 .

$\frac{1}{3}$ of them are yellow.

How many are yellow?

_____

Name _____

All in a Name

Work with a partner.
Draw lines to match each name tag to a cat.
Talk about how you named each cat.

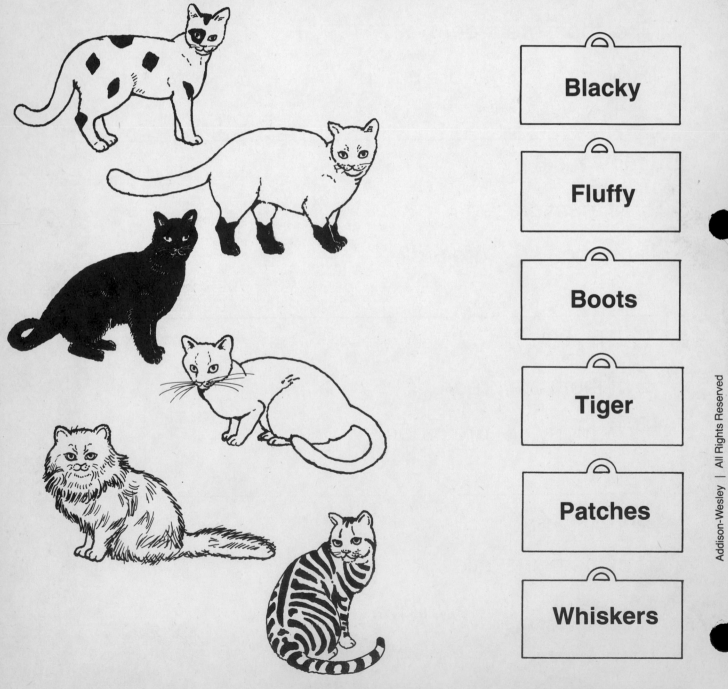

Blacky

Fluffy

Boots

Tiger

Patches

Whiskers